daybook, *n.* a book in which the events of the day are recorded; *specif.* a journal or diary

D A Y B O O K
of Critical Reading and Writing

FRAN CLAGGETT

LOUANN REID

RUTH VINZ

Great Source Education Group
a Houghton Mifflin Company
Wilmington, Massachusetts

www.greatsource.com

The Authors

Fran Claggett, currently an educational consultant for schools throughout the country and teacher at Sonoma State University, taught high school English for more than thirty years. She is author of several books, including *Drawing Your Own Conclusions: Graphic Strategies for Reading, Writing, and Thinking* (1992) and *A Measure of Success* (1996).

Louann Reid taught junior and senior high school English, speech, and drama for nineteen years and currently teaches courses for future English teachers at Colorado State University. Author of numerous articles and chapters, her first books were *Learning the Landscape* and *Recasting the Text* with Fran Claggett and Ruth Vinz (1996).

Ruth Vinz, currently a professor and director of English education at Teachers College, Columbia University, taught in secondary schools for twenty-three years. She is author of several books and numerous articles that discuss teaching and learning in the English classroom as well as a frequent presenter, consultant, and co-teacher in schools throughout the country.

Printed in the United States of America

International Standard Book Number: 0-669-46432-5

5 6 7 8 9 10 - RRDW - 04 03 02 01

3

4

5

Focus/Strategy	Lesson	Author/Literature

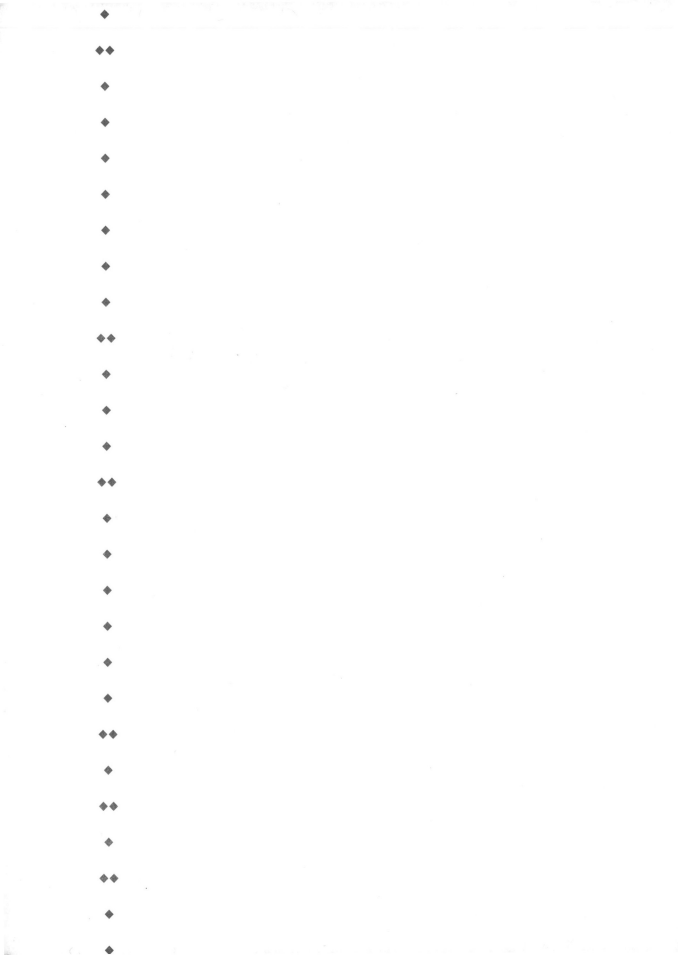

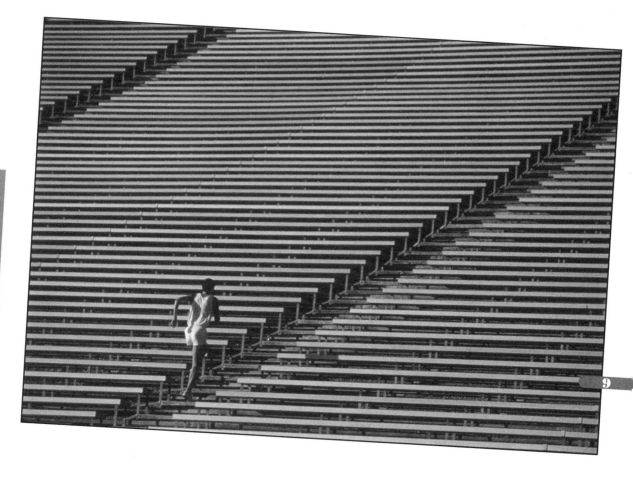

9

Angles of Literacy

What does it mean to be a "literate" person? Generally, we think of literate people as those who are able to read and write. But being literate also means that you can do whatever is required to communicate effectively. You may need to be able to draw diagrams, collaborate with others, listen carefully, or understand complex instructions.

The activities in this daybook emphasize five angles of literacy—five different ways to approach reading and writing. Strategies within each angle offer specific ways for you to read critically or write effectively. The angles are:

- interacting with a text
- making connections to the stories in a text
- shifting perspectives to examine a text from many points of view
- examining language and craft
- identifying biographical details

In this first unit, you will read poems by Nobel Prize-winning Irish poet Seamus Heaney from all five angles.

is important for readers to mark up what they are reading—in the margins and on the text itself. This is called **annotating**. Some things to do include:

- underlining key phrases
- writing questions or comments
- noting word patterns and repetitions
- circling words you do not know

As you read "Digging," notice how one reader has interacted with the text.

Response notes

Digging
Seamus Heaney

Between my finger and my thumb
The squat pen rests; snug as a gun.   *Why a gun?*

Son Present

Under my window, a clean rasping sound
When the spade sinks into gravelly ground:
My father, digging. I look down

20 years in the past

Till his straining rump among the flowerbeds
Bends low, comes up twenty years away
Stooping in rhythm through potato drills
Where he was digging.

Father

The coarse boot nestled on the lug, the shaft
Against the inside knee was levered firmly.
He rooted out tall tops, buried the bright edge deep
To scatter new potatoes that we picked
Loving their cool hardness in our hands.

By God, the old man could handle a spade.
Just like his old man.

Past

My grandfather cut more turf in a day
Than any other man on Toner's bog.
Once I carried him milk in a bottle
Corked sloppily with paper. He straightened up
To drink it, then fell to right away

Grandfather

Nicking and slicing neatly, heaving sods
Over his shoulder, going down and down
For the good turf. Digging.

Present

The cold smell of potato mould, the squelch and slap
Of soggy peat, the curt cuts of an edge
Through living roots awaken in my head.
But I've no spade to follow men like them.

Son

Between my finger and my thumb
The squat pen rests.
I'll dig with it.

In "Digging," Heaney begins in the present. The speaker of the poem is by his window, writing. He hears a sound and looks down to see his father digging. He remembers his father "twenty years away," digging potatoes. Next, he remembers that, as a child, he took his grandfather some milk while he was digging. The eighth stanza is a list of smells and sounds that "awaken in my head." But what is the significance of these incidents? They help connect him and his work—writing—with their work—digging. There's a sense that the speaker of the poem wants to labor with the skills with which his father and grandfather labored. And he is going to do so by writing.

Now, listen while someone reads "Blackberry-Picking" aloud. Remember to annotate the text as you listen.

Blackberry-Picking
Seamus Heaney

Response notes

for Philip Hobsbaum
Late August, given heavy rain and sun
For a full week, the blackberries would ripen.
At first, just one, a glossy purple clot
Among others, red, green, hard as a knot.
You ate that first one and its flesh was sweet
Like thickened wine: summer's blood was in it
Leaving stains upon the tongue and lust for
Picking. Then red ones inked up and that hunger
Sent us out with milk-cans, pea-tins, jam-pots
Where briars scratched and wet grass bleached our boots.
Round hayfields, cornfields and potato-drills
We trekked and picked until the cans were full,
Until the tinkling bottom had been covered
With green ones, and on top big dark blobs burned
Like a plate of eyes. Our hands were peppered
With thorn pricks, our palms sticky as Bluebeard's.

We hoarded the fresh berries in the byre.
But when the bath was filled we found a fur,
A rat-grey fungus, glutting on our cache.
The juice was stinking too. Once off the bush
The fruit fermented, the sweet flesh would turn sour.
I always felt like crying. It wasn't fair
That all the lovely canfuls smelt of rot.
Each year I hoped they'd keep, knew they would not.

●◆ Reread the poem silently. Then write a brief summary of the poem as you understand it so far. What is it about? What do you know about the speaker and the situation? Who do you suppose "we" and "our" refer to? Use examples from the text.

Story Connections

One way of reading and understanding texts is making story connections—looking at the stories being told or speculating on where the stories might have come from. When you make connections to the stories within literature, you will find that many texts contain experiences or incidents which are familiar to you. Strategies for making story connections include:

- noticing the stories being told
- connecting the stories to your own experience
- speculating on the meaning or significance of the incidents you find

Read the following poem and annotate the text.

Response notes

Mid-Term Break
Seamus Heaney

I sat all morning in the college sick bay
Counting bells knelling classes to a close.
At two o'clock our neighbours drove me home,

In the porch I met my father crying—
He had always taken funerals in his stride—
And Big Jim Evans saying it was a hard blow.

The baby cooed and laughed and rocked the pram
When I came in, and I was embarrassed
By old men standing up to shake my hand

And tell me they were 'sorry for my trouble';
Whispers informed strangers I was the eldest,
Away at school, as my mother held my hand

In hers and coughed out angry tearless sighs.
At ten o'clock the ambulance arrived
With the corpse, stanched and bandaged by the nurses.

Next morning I went up into the room. Snowdrops
And candles soothed the bedside; I saw him
For the first time in six weeks. Paler now,

Wearing a poppy bruise on his left temple,
He lay in the four foot box as in his cot.
No gaudy scars, the bumper knocked him clear.

A four foot box, a foot for every year.

First take a few minutes to write your initial impressions of this poem in the margin. Then discuss them with a partner, trying to reconstruct the events behind the poem. Imagine that you are an observer who does not know the family and you are reporting the events in the order they happened. List those events.

●◆Now, rewrite this poem as a news story, using the events you identified. Place the events in order of their importance, with the most important event first.

14

Experiences are remembered as stories. But these stories can be presented in many forms depending on the effect an author wants to create.

Discuss with a partner the differences in effect between telling the story as a list of events and as a poem. Which one includes more of the "events"? Which one creates a stronger feeling in the reader? Which one would you rather read and why?

Shifting **perspectives** means looking at what you read and write from many **points of view.** As good readers read, they form an idea about the meaning of the text. Then, they may try thinking about the text from other perspectives. A text may seem to mean one thing, but if you think about it another way, the meaning changes.

Authors select and shift perspectives when they write. They consider time, place, culture, or **genre** when creating a text. Active readers use several strategies for understanding the author's shifts:

- examining the point of view
- changing the point of view
- exploring various versions of an event
- forming interpretations
- comparing texts

Go back and reread "Mid-Term Break." Write down the point of view—that is, who is speaking in this poem? What can you infer about the speaker's age, relationship to the events, and feelings?

....

....

....

●◆ Change the point of view. Imagine that you are a neighbor telling a newspaper reporter about the accident. Write down a description of what happened from this point of view.

....

....

....

....

....

....

●◆ Compare your statement to the speaker's in the poem. Which is more emotional?

....

....

....

Look at a reading from several angles. Think about how changing the point of view changes the effect that the text has on a reader.

Studying an author's use of language will also help you understand a text. It is important to notice the words an author uses and the ways those words are arranged. There are many strategies you can use to pay attention to how a text is written as well as what it means:

- understanding figurative language
- looking at the way the author uses words
- modeling the style of other writers
- studying various kinds of literature

One kind of **figurative language** is **metaphor**. A metaphor is a **figure of speech** in which a writer implies that there are similarities between two or more unlike things, without directly stating what the comparison is. In "Digging," the pen is compared to both a gun and a shovel. Briefly discuss with a partner what qualities of each item help you understand the speaker's ideas. Read "Trout," paying attention to Heaney's choice of words and phrases.

Response notes

Trout
Seamus Heaney

Hangs, a fat gun-barrel,
deep under arched bridges
or slips like butter down
the throat of the river.

From depths smooth-skinned as
plums
his muzzle gets bull's eye;
picks off grass-seed and moths
that vanish, torpedoed.

Where water unravels
over gravel-beds he
is fired from the shallows
white belly reporting

flat; darts like a tracer-
bullet back between stones
and is never burnt out.
A volley of cold blood

ramrodding the current.

Heaney uses several comparisons to describe the trout. Some are **similes**, direct comparisons, using the word *like* or *as*. One is "darts like a tracer-bullet back between stones." He also uses metaphors such as "a fat gun-barrel."

Use a double-entry log to describe the comparisons in this poem. Jot down in the left column words or phrases that compare the trout or some aspect of the trout to something else. In the right column, write a few words explaining the implications of the comparison. What quality, for example, does "fat gun-barrel" suggest?

Words or phrases to compare the trout	Qualities implied by the comparison
"fat gun-barrel"	To me, "fat" suggests size and shape; "gun-barrel" suggests that the trout has the power and speed of a bullet.

17

Active reading requires paying close attention to how the words and structure of a text go together.

Focus on the Writer

By studying one writer in depth you can learn about an author's style. You can compare his or her prose and poetry and find patterns of images or ideas. You can also gain insights into a single text by knowing about the writer's life and work. For example, you might think that Heaney is describing his own life in Ireland in "Digging." Knowing that he grew up on a potato farm and his family cut peat from the surrounding bogs to build their fires suggests this. The land and connections to the past are very important to him.

Many strategies are available to help you focus on the writer:

- reading what the author says about writing, including where his or her ideas come from
- reading what others say about the author's writing
- making inferences about the connections between the author's life and work
- analyzing the author's style
- paying attention to repeated themes and topics in the work of the author

Reading a verbal collage gives you a chance to put the pieces of an author's life and work together. Collect information about Seamus Heaney by reading the quotations that follow. Make connections between the quotations and the poems you have read. Write your notes in the spaces around the quotations.

18

Heaney was born April 13, 1939, the eldest of nine children. He said in his 1995 Nobel Prize acceptance speech: "In the 1940s, when I was the eldest child of an ever-growing family in rural County Derry, we crowded together in the three rooms of a traditional thatched farmstead and lived a kind of den-life which was more or less emotionally and intellectually proofed against the outside world. It was an intimate, physical, creaturely existence in which the night sounds of the horse in the stable beyond one bedroom wall mingled with the sounds of adult conversation from the kitchen beyond the other. . . ."
from an interview with Seamus Heaney

"Commanding a great range of voices, idioms and metric conventions, Heaney's poetry nevertheless remains rooted in the soil of his native countryside, in the clash of ancient myth and modern politics, in domestic rituals and elegies for friends, family members, and those lost to sectarian violence in Northern Ireland. Despite his oft-invoked pet name, "Famous Seamus," Heaney prefers the solace of his phoneless Wicklow cottage and the toilsome pleasures of teaching to the glare of the limelight."
Jonathan Bing, from "Vindication of the word 'Poet'"

"His work is deeply rooted in the soil of his native land, in its mythology, its legends and its terrible beauty. In 14 volumes of poetry and prose, he has celebrated peat bogs and potato diggers, Ulster kings and ordinary farmers, using his 'squat pen' to dig up memories of his ancestral sod."
    from *The Boston Globe*, 10/06/95

"He has a particular sort of genius that even people who are not real readers of poetry can respond to. He reactivates the language every time he writes, even if he is just describing a bucket or a path in the woods."
    Sven Birkets

What connections do these quotations have with Seamus Heaney's poems? Where do you find critical or biographical details reflected in the poems or in something you wrote in the response notes about one of the poems? Record your answers in the chart.

Word or phrase from the collage	Word or phrase from a poem or from my response notes

Literate people—active readers and writers—know how important it is to reflect on what they learn. Take a moment to reflect now by looking back at the texts you have read by Seamus Heaney and the tentative conclusions you drew about them. Think about how reading the text from each angle of literacy, such as biography or language, helped you see certain aspects in the poem. Consider the processes you used as an active reader and writer.

●◆Now, apply those processes. Take any one poem in this cluster and focus on it from one angle. The angle should not be one that was used previously. For example, you might reread "Blackberry-Picking" from the angle of story connections or "Mid-Term Break" from the angle of language and craft. Explain in two or more paragraphs your interpretation of the poem from that angle and how looking at the poem in that way changed, even slightly, your initial understanding.

Knowing about a writer's life can help you understand his or her work. Use insights about a writer to help you read.

THE LESSONS STORIES TEACH

© 1998 GREAT SOURCE. ALL RIGHTS RESERVED.

The Lessons Stories Teach

Whether it is true or not, the story told about George Washington chopping down the cherry tree teaches a lesson about the importance of telling the truth. Stories are one medium through which we learn to make sense of the world around us. They are passed from generation to generation and record the larger story of how we have come to understand ourselves and our world.

Certain stories are such a part of our culture that they are *archetypal*— the original model after which other things are patterned. For example, the parable of the prodigal son from the Bible is an archetypal story. It tells of a young man who wastes his inheritance but is forgiven by his father when he returns home. The story teaches us about forgiveness and the importance of family.

The parable has been told in many versions, but the basic pattern of events stays the same. It has become a motif, an idea used symbolically in other works of literature.

Many stories offer of interpreting and organizing experience. They require the reader to work from two places at once. First, readers locate themselves in the pattern of action in the story, noticing what is going on. Simultaneously, they construct and develop formulations about the significance of the pattern—the lessons that the story teaches. The story of King Midas from classical mythology is structured in such a pattern.

Response notes

The Story of Midas from *The Metamorphoses*
Ovid, translated by Rolfe Humphries

. . . .And Bacchus,
Happy and grateful, and meaning well, told Midas
To make his choice of anything he wanted.
And Midas, never too judicious, answered:
"Grant that whatever I touch may turn to gold!"
Bacchus agreed, gave him the ruinous gift,
Sorry the monarch had not chosen better.
So Midas went his cheerful way, rejoicing
In his own bad luck, and tried to test the promise
By touching this and that. It all was true,
He hardly dared believe it! From an oak-tree
He broke a green twig loose: the twig was golden.
He picked a stone up from the ground; the stone
Paled with light golden color; he touched a clod,
The clod became a nugget. Awns of grain
Were a golden harvest; if he picked an apple
It seemed a gift from the Hesperides.
He placed his fingers on the lofty pillars
And saw them gleam and shine. He bathed his hands
In water, and the stream was golden rain
Like that which came to Danae. His mind
Could scarcely grasp his hopes—all things were golden,
Or would be, at his will! A happy man,
He watched his servants set a table before him
With bread and meat. He touched the gift of Ceres
And found it stiff and hard; he tried to bite
The meat with hungry teeth, and where the teeth
Touched food they seemed to touch on golden ingots.
He mingled water with the wine of Bacchus;
It was molten gold that trickled through his jaws.

Midas, astonished at his new misfortune,
Rich man and poor man, tries to flee his riches
Hating the favor he had lately prayed for.
No food relieves his hunger; his throat is dry

With burning thirst; he is tortured, as he should be,
By the hateful gold. Lifting his hands to Heaven,
He cries: "Forgive me, father! I have sinned.
Have mercy upon me, save me from this loss
That looks so much like gain!" The gods are kind,
And Bacchus, since he owned his fault, forgave him,
Took back the gift. "You need not be forever
Smeared with that foolish color: go to the stream
That flows by Sardis, take your way upstream
Into the Lydian hills, until you find
The tumbling river's source. There duck your head
And body under the foaming white of the fountain,
And wash your sin away." The king obeyed him,
And the power of the golden touch imbued the water,
So that even now the fields grow hard and yellow
If that vein washes over them to flood
Their fields with the water of the touch of gold.

List the key events that make up the action in the story.

....

....

....

....

....

....

....

●◆ Write a statement about the lessons this story teaches—that is, the
significance of the action.

....

....

....

....

© GREAT SOURCE ALL RIG

...ite an updated and very short story using the pattern—wish made, granted, and then regretted—that is basic to the Midas story. The details you include should emphasize the lesson you want to teach your reader.

Symbolic Meaning

Within the patterns that organize a story are symbols that illustrate or extend meaning. **Symbols** identify one thing with another. In the story of Midas, gold is a symbol of greed. Midas' journey to the river's source may symbolize his need to cleanse himself of greed. Symbols are a shorthand of sorts. In the following excerpt, the philosopher Erich Fromm explains how ideas and objects take on symbolic meaning.

from **"The Nature of Symbolic Language"** by Erich Fromm

Take, for instance, the symbol of fire. We are fascinated by certain qualities of fire in a fireplace. First of all, by its aliveness. It changes continuously, it moves all the time, and yet there is a constancy in it. It remains the same without being the same. It gives the impression of power, of energy, of grace and lightness. It is as if it were dancing and had an inexhaustible source of energy. When we use fire as a symbol, we describe the inner experience characterized by the same elements which we notice in the sensory experience of fire; the mood of energy, lightness, movement, grace, gaiety—sometimes one, sometimes another of these elements being predominant in the feeling. . . .

If we watch fire in the fireplace, which is a source of pleasure and comfort, it is expressive of a mood of aliveness, warmth, and pleasure. But if we see a building or forest on fire, it conveys to us an experience of threat or terror, of the powerlessness of man against the elements of nature. Fire, then, can be the symbolic representation of inner aliveness and happiness as well as of fear, powerlessness, or of one's own destructive tendencies.

←——Response notes——→

25

In the center circle put one word that has symbolic meaning to you. List the characteristics you associate with the symbol in the additional circles. On each spoke between the circles, suggest the symbolic meaning associated with that characteristic.

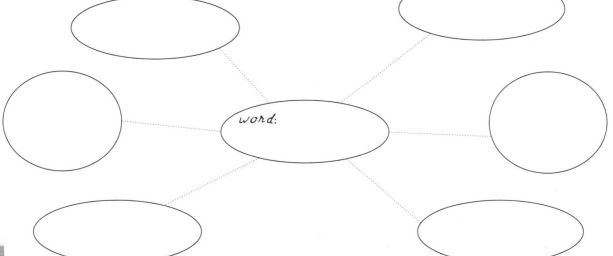

word:

Now that you have worked through the characteristics of one symbol, see if you can explain the use of symbol in the following poem written by the Russian poet Andrei Voznesensky.

Response notes

First Frost
Andrei Voznesensky

A girl is freezing in a telephone booth,
huddled in her flimsy coat,

her face stained by tears
and smeared with lipstick.

She breathes on her thin little fingers.
Fingers like ice. Glass beads in her ears.

She has to beat her way back alone
down the icy street.

First frost. A beginning of losses.
The first frost of telephone phrases.

It is the start of winter glittering on her cheek,
the first frost of having been hurt.

●◆ Circle phrases and images in the poem that you associate with the title. Then, write an explanation of how the title of the poem and its symbolism link the sensory details with a larger emotional meaning.

....

....

....

....

....

....

....

....

Symbols are used to show the connections between the physical world (sensory) and the world of the mind (emotional and intellectual).

Three
Understanding New Symbols

In the story of Midas and in "First Frost," symbols are used to make imaginative connections between physical and emotional worlds. Gold and frost are common symbols that you may have seen before. But sometimes the symbols used are outside your range of experiences. This is particularly true if the story is written by an author from a culture other than your own. Then, you must let the story and its author instruct you. The opening paragraphs of the following story by Leslie Marmon Silko may require you to infer symbolic meaning from the ritual she describes.

from **"The Man to Send Rain Clouds"** by Leslie Marmon Silko

←—Response notes—→

They found him under a big cottonwood tree. His Levi jacket and pants were faded light-blue so that he had been easy to find. The big cottonwood tree stood apart from a small grove of winterbare cottonwoods which grew in the wide, sandy arroyo. He had been dead for a day or more, and the sheep had wandered and scattered up and down the arroyo. Leon and his brother-in-law, Ken, gathered the sheep and left them in the pen at the sheep camp before they returned to the cottonwood tree. Leon waited under the tree while Ken drove the truck through the deep sand to the edge of the arroyo. He squinted up at the sun and unzipped his jacket—it sure was hot for this time of year. But high and northwest the blue mountains were still deep in snow. Ken came sliding down the low, crumbling bank about fifty yards down, and he was bringing the red blanket.

Before they wrapped the old man, Leon took a piece of string out of his pocket and tied a small gray feather in the old man's long white hair. Ken gave him the paint. Across the brown wrinkled forehead he drew a streak of white and along the high cheekbones he drew a strip of blue paint. He paused and watched Ken throw pinches of corn meal and pollen into the wind that fluttered the small gray feather. Then Leon painted with yellow under the old man's broad nose, and finally, when he had painted green across the chin, he smiled.

"Send us rain clouds, Grandfather." They laid the bundle in the back of the pickup and covered it with a heavy tarp before they started back to the pueblo.

They turned off the highway onto the sandy pueblo road. Not long after they passed the store and post office they saw Father Paul's car coming toward them. When he recognized their faces he slowed his car and waved for them to stop. The young priest rolled down the car window.

"Did you find old Teofilo?" he asked loudly.

Leon stopped the truck. "Good morning, Father. We were just out to the sheep camp. Everything is O.K. now."

"Thank God for that. Teofilo is a very old man. You really shouldn't allow him to stay at the sheep camp alone."

"No, he won't do that any more now."

from **"The Man to Send Rain Clouds"** by Leslie Marmon Silko

← Response notes →

"Well, I'm glad you understand. I hope I'll be seeing you at Mass this week—we missed you last Sunday. See if you can get old Teofilo to come with you." The priest smiled and waved at them as they drove away.

Silko said of herself: "What I know is Laguna. This place I am from is everything I am as a writer and human being." Obviously, Silko understands the significance of the ritual she describes. How can you, as a reader, infer meaning from Ken's and Leon's actions and the objects associated with the ritual surrounding Teofilo's death? An **inference** is any reasonable conclusion that is based on the evidence provided. Fill in the chart below as a preparation for writing a short essay.

ACTIONS AND OBJECTS	SYMBOLIC CONNECTION	INFERRED MEANING
feather tied in hair	feather=flight or freedom	aid Teofilo's journey to afterlife

© GREAT SOURCE. ALL RIGHTS RESERVED.

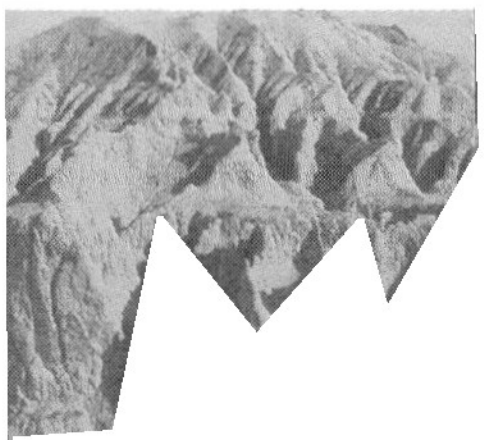

●◆ Write a short essay describing what you think the symbols in Silko's story mean. Describe the inferences you made to arrive at these conclusions.

29

Noticing details
the literal level, connecting

Four

Familiar Symbols in Unfamiliar Places

E ven in stories of imaginary future worlds, you will find familiar symbols. Read the following story by Ray Bradbury about life on Mars in the year 2001. Bradbury offers you a chance to enter an entirely new world, but one filled with familiar symbols.

"December 2001: The Green Morning" by Ray Bradbury

← Response notes →

When the sun set, he crouched by the path and cooked a small supper and listened to the fire crack while he put the food in his mouth and chewed thoughtfully. It had been a day not unlike thirty others, with many neat holes dug in the dawn hours, seeds dropped in, and water brought from the bright canals. Now, with an iron weariness in his slight body, he lay and watched the sky color from one darkness to another.

His name was Benjamin Driscoll, and he was thirty-one-years old. And the thing that he wanted was Mars grown green and tall with trees and foliage, producing air, more air, growing larger with each season; trees to cool the towns in the boiling summer, trees to hold back the winter winds. There were so many things a tree could do: add color, provide shade, drop fruit, or become a children's playground, a whole sky universe to climb and hang from; an architecture of food and pleasure, that was a tree. But most of all the trees would distill an icy air for the lungs, and a gentle rustling for the ear when you lay nights in your snowy bed and were gentled to sleep by the sound.

He lay listening to the dark earth gather itself, waiting for the sun, for the rains that hadn't come yet. His ear to the ground, he could hear the feet of the years ahead moving at a distance, and he imagined the seeds he had placed today sprouting up with green and taking hold on the sky, pushing out branch after branch, until Mars was an afternoon forest, Mars was a shining orchard.

In the early morning, with the small sun lifting faintly among the folded hills, he would be up and finished with a smoky breakfast in a few minutes and, trodding out the fire ashes, be on his way with knapsacks, testing, digging, placing seed or sprout, tamping lightly, watering, going on, whistling, looking at the clear sky brightening toward a warm noon.

"You need the air," he told his night fire. The fire was a ruddy, lively companion that snapped back at you, that slept close by with drowsy pink eyes warm through the chilly night. "We all need the air. It's a thin air here on Mars. You get tired so soon. It's like living in the Andes, in South America, high. You inhale and don't get anything. It doesn't satisfy."

He felt his rib cage. In thirty days, how it had grown. To take in more air, they would all have to build their lungs. Or plant more trees.

"That's what I'm here for," he said. The fire popped. "In school they told a story about Johnny Appleseed walking across America planting apple trees. Well, I'm doing more. I'm planting oaks, elms,

"December 2001: The Green Morning" by Ray Bradbury

and maples, every kind of tree, aspens and deodars, and chestnuts. Instead of making just fruit for the stomach, I'm making air for the lungs. When those trees grow up some year, *think* of the oxygen they'll make!"

He remembered his arrival on Mars. Like a thousand others, he had gazed out upon a still morning and thought, How do I fit here? What will I do? Is there a job for me?

Then he had fainted.

Someone pushed a vial of ammonia to his nose and, coughing, he came around.

"You'll be all right," said the doctor.

"What happened?"

"The air's pretty thin. Some can't take it. I think you'll have to go back to earth."

"No!" He sat up and almost immediately felt his eyes darken and Mars revolve twice around under him. His nostrils dilated and he forced his lungs to drink in deep nothingnesses. "I'll be all right. I've got to stay here!"

They let him lie gasping in horrid fishlike motions. And he thought, Air, air, air. They're sending me back because of air. And he turned his head to look across the Martian fields and hills. He brought them to focus, and the first thing he noticed was that there were no trees, no trees at all, as far as you could look in any direction. The land was down upon itself, a land of black loam, but nothing on it, not even grass. Air, he thought, the thin stuff whistling in his nostrils. Air, air. And on top of hills, or in their shadows, or even by little creeks, not a tree and not a single green blade of grass. Of course! He felt the answer came not from his mind, but his lungs and his throat. And the thought was like a sudden gust of pure oxygen, raising him up. Trees and grass. He looked down at his hands and turned them over. He would plant trees and grass. That would be his job, to fight against the very thing that might prevent his staying here. He would have a private horticultural war with Mars. There lay the old soil, and the plants of it so ancient they had worn themselves out. But what if new forms were introduced? Earth trees, great mimosas and weeping willows and magnolias and magnificent eucalyptus. What then? There was no guessing what mineral wealth hid in the soil, untapped because the old ferns, flowers, bushes, and trees had tired themselves to death.

"Let me up!" he shouted. "I've got to see the Coordinator!"
He and the Coordinator had talked an entire morning about things that grew and were green. It would be months, if not years, before organized planting began. So far, frosted food was brought from earth in flying icicles; a few community gardeners were greening up in hydroponic plants.

"Meanwhile," said the Coordinator, "it's your job. We'll get what seed we can for you, a little equipment. Space on the rockets is mighty precious now. I'm afraid, since these first towns are mining communities, there won't be much sympathy for your tree planting—"

"But you'll let me do it?"

They let him do it. Provided with a single motorcycle, its bin full of rich seeds and sprouts, he had parked his vehicle in the valley wilderness and struck out on foot over the land.

That had been thirty days ago, and he had never glanced back. For looking back would have been sickening to the heart. The weather was excessively dry; it was doubtful if any seeds had sprouted yet. Perhaps his entire campaign, his four weeks of bending and scooping were lost. He kept his eyes only ahead of him, going on down this wide shallow valley under the sun, away from First Town, waiting for the rains to come.

Clouds were gathering over the dry mountains now as he drew his blanket over his shoulders. Mars was a place as unpredictable as time. He felt the baked hills simmering down into frosty night, and he thought of the rich, inky soil, a soil so black and shiny it almost crawled and stirred in your fist, a rank soil from which might sprout gigantic beanstalks from which, with bone-shaking concussion, might drop screaming giants.

The fire fluttered into sleepy ash. The air tremored to the distant roll of a cartwheel. Thunder. A sudden odor of water. Tonight, he thought, and put his hand out to feel for rain. Tonight.

He awoke to a tap on his brow.

Water ran down his nose into his lips. Another drop hit his eye, blurring it. Another splashed his chin.

The rain.

Raw, gentle, and easy, it mizzled out of the high air, a special elixir, tasting of spells and stars and air, carrying a peppery dust in it, and moving like a rare light sherry on his tongue.

Rain.

He sat up. He let the blanket fall and his blue denim shirt spot, while the rain took on more solid drops. The first looked as though an invisible animal were dancing on it, crushing it, until it was angry smoke. The rain fell. The great black lid of sky cracked in six powdery blue chips, like a marvelous crackled glaze, and rushed down. He saw ten billion rain crystals, hesitating long enough to be photographed by the electrical display. Then darkness and water. He was drenched to the skin, but he held his face up and let the water hit his eyelids, laughing. He clapped his hands together and stepped up and walked around his little camp, and it was one o'clock in the morning.

It rained steadily for two hours and then stopped. The stars came out, freshly washed and clearer than ever.

Changing into dry clothes from his cellophane pack, Mr. Benjamin Driscoll lay down and went happily to sleep.

The sun rose slowly among the hills. It broke out upon the land quietly and wakened Mr. Driscoll where he lay.

He waited a moment before arising. He had worked and waited a long hot month, and now, standing up, he turned at last and faced the direction from which he had come.

It was a green morning.

32

"December 2001: The Green Morning" by Ray Bradbury

← Response notes →

As far as he could see the trees were standing up against the sky. Not one tree, not two, not a dozen, but the thousands he had planted in seed and sprout. And not little trees, no, not saplings, not little tender shoots, but great trees, huge trees, trees as tall as ten men, green and huge and round and full, trees shimmering their metallic leaves, trees whispering, trees in a line over hills, lemon trees, lime trees, redwood and mimosas and oaks and elms and aspens, cherry, maple, ash, apple, orange, eucalyptus, stung by a tumultuous rain, nourished by alien and magical soil and, even as he watched, throwing out new branches, popping open new buds.

"Impossible!" cried Mr. Benjamin Driscoll.

But the valley and the morning were green.

And the air!

All about, like a moving current, a mountain river, came the new air, the oxygen blowing from the green trees. You could see it shimmer high in crystal billows. Oxygen, fresh, pure, green, cold oxygen turning the valley into a river delta. In a moment the town doors would flip wide, people would run out through the new miracle of oxygen, sniffing, gusting in lungfuls of it, cheeks pinking with it, noses frozen with it, lungs revivified, hearts leaping, and worn bodies lifted into a dance.

Mr. Benjamin Driscoll took one long deep drink of green water and air and fainted.

Before he woke again five thousand new trees had climbed up into the yellow sun.

33

Look back at the story and circle anything in the text that you think has symbolic meaning. List the symbols you find in the chart below. In the middle column, describe the characteristics of the symbol. In the right column, explain how the symbol is connected to the title of the story.

SYMBOLS	CHARACTERISTICS	CONNECTIONS TO TITLE
seeds	possibility of life, abundance	seeds = possibility of growth, of green

What does the character Benjamin Driscoll symbolize in the story? For example, references are made to Johnny Appleseed and the beanstalk story. In order to portray your understanding of him as a symbol, draw a series of frames that depict the various actions that he takes on Mars. End with a frame that predicts the action he will take after he wakes up from his faint.

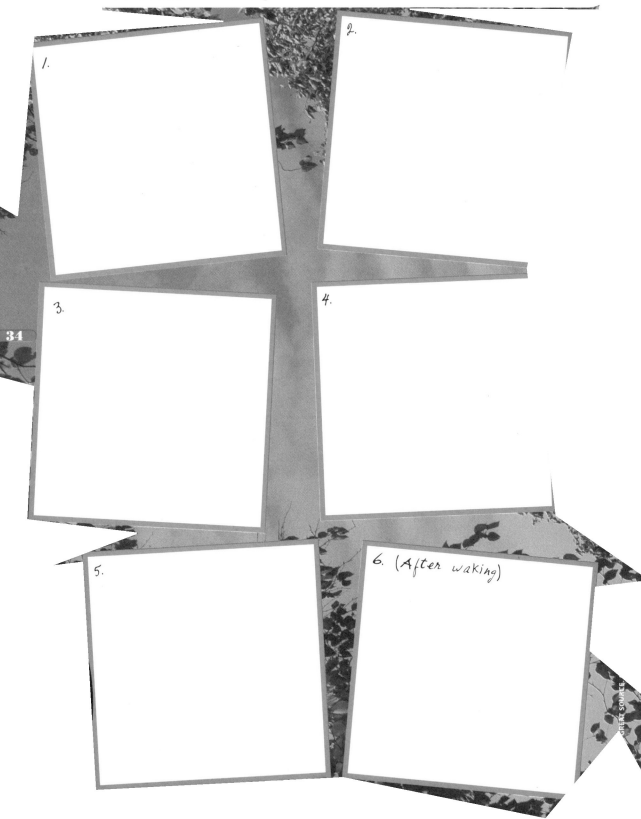

1.

2.

3.

4.

5.

6. (After waking)

Five

A Network of Symbols in Story

Some writers use a network of symbols to illustrate multiple themes or underlying conflicts in their stories. For example, Bradbury has symbols of fertility—seeds, sprouts, and "rich inky soil"—along with symbols that represent barrenness— dryness, "frosty nights," and darkness. What might this unlikely pairing mean? As a way to understand the network of symbols that link various themes and ideas together in Bradbury's story, it might be helpful to create a visual map that shows the network of symbols in the story.

Fill in the web below with categories of symbols—for example, fertility or barrenness as mentioned above. Some categories will overlap. Fill in the lines with a word or phrase that describes the category.

growth
"sprouting"
green

water, rain
"seeds dropped in"
"rich inky soil"
fertility

Write about what you think will happen now that "five thousand new trees had climbed up into the yellow sun"? What do you think the story has to teach us about colonization and development on other planets?

●◆ Write a continuation of Bradbury's story. Incorporate the symbols that he has introduced as well as any you want to add that will further the meaning.

36

Heroes and Heroines

The heroes and heroines in literature are often "larger than life" characters who possess extraordinary qualities. Jason had to tame wild bulls, sow the teeth of a serpent, and kill a dragon in order to acquire the Golden Fleece and return it to its rightful place. Rapunzel restored the vision of the blind prince with her tears. Heroes and heroines embody qualities of character we might all like to possess—self-control, endurance, imagination, vision, intelligence, etc. Our ideals have evolved over time, and it is possible to trace this evolution in the portrayal of heroes and heroines. How have the dragon-slaying hero and the heroine as protector of men changed in modern versions? How do contemporary authors depict heroes or heroines?

Who are your heroes and heroines?

Who Is a Hero?

The qualities that are associated with a hero vary widely across time and place. The characteristics are not clear-cut as creating a list of your own will show. Make a list of seven men from film, literature, or the real world whom you would call a hero. List the characteristics of each that make the person a hero in your view.

Name	Characteristics

➡️ Compare your chart with the charts of others. Then collaborate on a list of the qualities of character and the deeds you associate with a hero of today.

Heroes may attain their goals or die while trying. Whatever the outcome, they appear larger-than-life in most accounts. While the symbolic idea of the hero endures across time, it's interesting to consider how or if the ideal type changes. The very ancient story of Beowulf is a reminder of the roots of the tradition of the hero in our cultural conceptions. Note particularly how the qualities of character that Beowulf reveals about himself compare with the heroes you named in your list.

from *Beowulf*
translated by Burton Raffel

Beowulf answered, Edgetho's great son.
"Ah! Unferth, my friend, your face
Is hot with ale, and your tongue has tried
To tell us about Brecca's doings. But the truth
Is simple: no man swims in the sea
As I can, no strength is a match for mine.
As boys, Brecca and I had boasted—
We were both too young to know better—that we'd risk
Our lives far out at sea, and so
We did. Each of us carried a naked
Sword, prepared for whales or the swift
Sharp teeth and beaks of needlefish.
He could never leave me behind, swim faster
Across the waves than I could, and I
Had chosen to remain close to his side.
I remained near him for five long nights,
Until a flood swept us apart;
The frozen sea surged around me,
It grew dark, the wind turned bitter, blowing
From the north, and the waves were savage. Creatures
Who sleep deep in the sea were stirred
Into life—and the iron hammered links
On my mail shirt, these shining bits of metal
Woven across my breast, saved me
From death. A monster seized me, drew me
Swiftly toward the bottom, swimming with its claws
Tight in my flesh. But fate let me
Find its heart with my sword, hack myself
Free; I fought that beast's last battle,
Left it floating lifeless in the sea.
"Other monsters crowded around me,
Continually attacking. I treated them politely,
Offering the edge of my razor-sharp sword. But the feast,
I think, did not please them, filled
Their evil bellies with no banquet-rich food,
Thrashing there at the bottom of the sea;
By morning they'd decided to sleep on the shore,
Lying on their backs, their blood spilled out
On the sand. Afterward, sailors could cross
That sea-road and feel no fear; nothing
Would stop their passing. Then God's bright beacon
Appeared in the east, the water lay still,
And at last I could see the land, wind-swept

Response notes

39

FROM **BEOWULF** (continued)

Cliff walls at the edge of the coast. Fate saves
The living when they drive away death by themselves!
Lucky or not, nine was the number
Of sea-huge monsters I killed. What man,
Anywhere under Heaven's high arch, has fought
In such darkness, endured more misery or been harder
Pressed? Yet I survived the sea, smashed
The monsters' hot jaws, swam home from my journey.
The swift-flowing waters swept me along
And I landed on Finnish soil. I've heard
No tales of you, Unferth, telling
Of such clashing terror, such contests in the night!
Brecca's battles were never so bold;
Neither he nor you can match me—and I mean
No boast, have announced no more than I know
To be true."

●◆ Choose one of the heroes from your list and write a speech like Beowulf's for him. Have him tell a story about himself (a boast similar to Beowulf's) that reveals qualities of character or deeds of a contemporary hero.

●◆ What do you see as the main differences in the qualities of a hero of Beowulf's time and a contemporary one (as demonstrated in your speech).

Who Is a Heroine?

What are the qualities you associate with a heroine? Many of the most celebrated women in history are portrayed as temptresses—Eve, Helen of Troy, and Cleopatra. Are these the sort of women you would consider heroines?

Make a list of seven women from film, literature, or the real world who you would call heroines. List the characteristics of each that make them a heroine in your view.

Name	Characteristics

42

Compare lists with others and determine the qualities of character of a heroine. Then compare this list with the one you made for a hero in lesson one. Make a Venn diagram to show the differences and similarities between your view of a hero and a heroine.

hero   heroine

In the ancient Greek epic poem *The Odyssey*, the goddess Circe tells the hero Odysseus about the trials he will face at sea. She offers him advice and instruction on how to overcome the difficulties. In doing so, she reveals some of the characteristics of the heroine in classical literature. How do her deeds compare with the qualities of heroines that you listed?

Response notes

from **The Odyssey**
Homer
translated by Robert Fitzgerald

                              "A second course
lies between headlands. One is a sharp mountain
piercing the sky, with stormcloud round the peak
dissolving never, not in the brightest summer,
to show heaven's azure there, nor in the fall.
No mortal man could scale it, nor so much
as land there, not with twenty hands and feet,
so sheer the cliffs are—as of polished stone.
Midway that height, a cavern full of mist
opens toward Erebos and evening. Skirting
this in the lugger, great Odysseus,
your master bowman, shooting from the deck,
would come short of the cavemouth with his shaft;
but that is the den of Scylla, where she yaps
abominably, a newborn whelp's cry,
though she is huge and monstrous. God or man,
no one could look on her in joy. Her legs—
and there are twelve—are like great tentacles,
unjointed, and upon her serpent necks
are borne six heads like nightmares of ferocity,
with triple serried rows of fangs and deep
gullets of black death. Half her length, she sways
her heads in air, outside her horrid cleft,
hunting the sea around that promontory
for dolphins, dogfish, or what bigger game
thundering Amphitrite feeds in thousands.
And no ship's company can claim
to have passed her without loss and grief; she takes,
from every ship, one man for every gullet.

"The opposite point seems more a tongue of land
you'd touch with a good bowshot, at the narrows.
A great wild fig, a shaggy mass of leaves,
grows on it, and Charybdis lurks below
to swallow down the dark sea tide. Three times
from dawn to dusk she spews it up
and sucks it down again three times, a swirling
maelstrom; if you come upon her then
the god who makes earth tremble could not save you.
No, hug the cliff of Scylla, take your ship
through on a racing stroke. Better to mourn

43

six men than lose them all, and the ship, too."
So her advice ran; but I faced her, saying:
"Only instruct me, goddess, if you will,
how, if possible, can I pass Charybdis,
or fight off Scylla when she raids my crew?"

Swiftly that loveliest goddess answered me:

"Must you have battle in your heart forever?
The bloody toil of combat? Old contender,
will you not yield to the immortal gods?
That nightmare cannot die, being eternal
evil itself—horror, and pain, and chaos;
there is no fighting her, no power can fight her,
all that avails is flight."

In the song "Lady Madonna," John Lennon and Paul McCartney create a portrait of another type of heroine. How does this woman's qualities compare with those you listed ?

Lady Madonna
John Lennon and Paul McCartney

Lady Madonna children at your feet
wonder how you manage to make ends meet.
Who finds the money when you pay the rent?
Did you think that money was heaven sent?
Friday night arrives without a suitcase
Sunday morning creeps in like a nun
Monday's child has learned to tie his bootlace.
See how they'll run.
Lady Madonna baby at your breast
wonder how you manage to feed the rest.
See how they'll run.
Lady Madonna lying on the bed
listen to the music playing in your head.
Tuesday afternoon is never ending
Wedn'sday morning papers didn't come
Thursday night your stockings needed mending.
See how they'll run.
Lady Madonna children at your feet
wonder how you manage to make ends meet.

●◆ Create a dialogue between Circe and Lady Madonna discussing the qualities that they admire in women. In your dialogue, have each reveal the name of one woman she would consider a heroine and have her explain why.

Heroines
in literature
are symbolic of
the qualities of
character that
were admired in
women in
different time
periods and
places.

In a short essay, the novelist Alice Walker described how the nineteenth-century rights-crusader Sojourner Truth served as a model of commitment and action for her life. A former slave, Sojourner Truth chose her name because it represented what she believed was her calling in life. She traveled the country lecturing about the rights of African Americans and women.

"A Name Is Sometimes An Ancestor Saying HI, I'm With You"
by Alice Walker

←——Response notes——→

There are always people in history (or herstory) who help us, and whose "job" it is, in fact, to do this. One way of looking at history (whether oral or written) is as a method that records characteristics and vibrations of our helpers, whose spirits we may feel but of whose objective reality as people who once lived we may not know. Now these people—our "spirit helpers," as indigenous peoples time after time in all cultures have referred to them—always create opportunities that make a meeting with and recognition of them unavoidable.

Sojourner Truth is one such figure for me. Even laying aside such obvious resemblances as the fact that we are both as concerned about the rights of women as the rights of men, and that we share a certain "mystical" bent, Sojourner ("Walker"—in the sense of traveler, journeyer, wanderer) Truth (which "Alice" means in Old Greek) is also my name. How happy I was when I realized this. It is one of those "synchronicities" (some might say conceits) of such reassuring proportions that even when I've been tempted to rename myself "Treeflower" or "Weed" I have resisted.

I get a power from this name that Sojourner Truth and I share. And when I walk into a room of strangers who are hostile to the words of women, I do so with her/our cloak of authority—as black women and beloved expressions of the Universe (i.e., children of God)—warm about me.

She smiles within my smile. That irrepressible great heart rises in my chest. Every experience that roused her passion against injustice in her lifetime shines from my eyes.

This feeling of being loved and supported by the Universe in general and by certain recognizable spirits in particular is bliss. No other state is remotely like it. And perhaps that is what Jesus tried so hard to teach: that the transformation required of us is not simply to be "like" Christ, but to be Christ.

The spirit of our helpers incarnates in us, making us more ourselves by extending us far beyond. And to that spirit there is no "beginning" as we know it (although we might finally "know" a historical figure who at one time expressed it) and no end. Always a hello, from the concerned spiritual ancestor you may not even have known you had—but this could strike at any time. Never a good-bye.

Circle or highlight with a marker the qualities of character in Sojourner Truth that Walker suggests have become her own.

46

◉◆ Write your own "A Name Is Sometimes An Ancestor" essay. Who
has served as a model of conduct for you? What are the important
things this person has taught you?

Heroes and
heroines are a
major influence for
good in people's lives,
providing examples of
action, commitment,
and belief.

Heroes and heroines teach us something about ourselves and provide models of how to live. But, it is important to question just what any individual **characterization** represents, to question and challenge what the heroes and heroines represent. Louise Erdrich chose to do this through a poem.

Dear John Wayne
Louise Erdrich

August and the drive-in picture is packed.
We lounge on the hood of the Pontiac
surrounded by the slow-burning spirals they sell
at the window, to vanquish the hordes of mosquitoes.
Nothing works. They break through the smoke-screen for blood.

Always the look-out spots the Indians first,
spread north to south, barring progress.
The Sioux, or Cheyenne, or some bunch in spectacular columns,
arranged like SAC missiles,
their feathers bristling in the meaningful sunset.

The drum breaks. There will be no parlance.
Only the arrows whining, a death-cloud of nerves
swarming down on the settlers
who die beautifully, tumbling like dust weeds
into the history that brought us all here
together: this wide screen beneath the sign of the bear.

The sky fills, acres of blue squint and eye
that the crowd cheers. His face moves over us,
a thick cloud of vengeance, pitted
like the land that was once flesh. Each rut,
each scar makes a promise: *It is
not over, this fight, not as long as you resist.*

Everything we see belongs to us.
A few laughing Indians fall over the hood
slipping in the hot spilled butter.
The eye sees a lot, John, but the heart is so blind.
How will you know what you own?
He smiles, a horizon of teeth
the credits reel over, and then the white fields
again blowing in the true-to-life dark.
The dark films over everything.
We get into the car
scratching our mosquito bites, speechless and small
as people are when the movie is done.
We are back in ourselves.

48

How can we help but keep hearing his voice,
the flip side of the sound-track, still playing:
Come on, boys, we've got them
where we want them, drunk, running.
They will give us what we want, what we need:
The heart is a strange wood inside of everything
we see, burning, doubling, splitting out of its skin.

Response notes

You may have seen John Wayne in a movie at some time. He is best known for his role as the tough hero of westerns. In the films, he often fought against Native American tribes who did not want to give up their homelands. Louise Erdrich is of Native American ancestry, so she brings a critical eye to the consideration of a figure like John Wayne. Notice how the alternating voices of her poem—moving back and forth between the Native Americans watching the movie and the actions and dialogue of John Wayne in the movie—emphasize how his status as a cultural hero may have negative effects.

Use a different color of ink to mark off each of the alternating perspectives in the poem—the movie, the moviegoers, and the poet's reflections.

●◆ Reread each section you marked. Then, write about the main ideas expressed in each and what images you think are the most powerful in making the points.

49

Movie:

Moviegoers:

Reflections:

●◆ Now, think of a hero or heroine whose actions might be viewed with a critical eye by someone else. Write a poem, using Erdrich's structure as a model, in which you question the qualities of character generally regarded as admirable.

Writers not only create characterizations of heroes and heroines, but also question or challenge the representations that have been made by others.

Five Who Are My Heroes or Heroines?

The writer Robert Hayden created a portrait of one of his heroes, Frederick Douglass, in the following poem. Douglass, who lived in the 1800s, was honored by President Lincoln for his efforts to recruit black soldiers to fight in the Union Army during the Civil War. As you read, note qualities of character that seem to distinguish Douglass.

Frederick Douglass
Robert Hayden

When it is finally ours, this freedom, this liberty, this beautiful
and terrible thing, needful to man as air,
usable as earth; when it belongs at last to all,
when it is truly instinct, brain matter, diastole, systole,
reflex action; when it is finally won; when it is more
than the gaudy mumbo jumbo of politicians:
this man, this Douglass, this former slave, this Negro
beaten to his knees, exiled, visioning a world
where none is lonely, none hunted, alien,
this man, superb in love and logic, this man
shall be remembered. Oh, not with statues' rhetoric,
not with legends and poems and wreaths of bronze alone,
but with the lives grown out of his life, the lives
fleshing his dream of the beautiful, needful thing.

Response Notes

51

Use the cluster below to examine the qualities of one of your heroes or heroines. Put the name in the center circle. Fill in the next circles with the qualities of character or deeds you admire. In the outer circles list reasons why you value these qualities or actions.

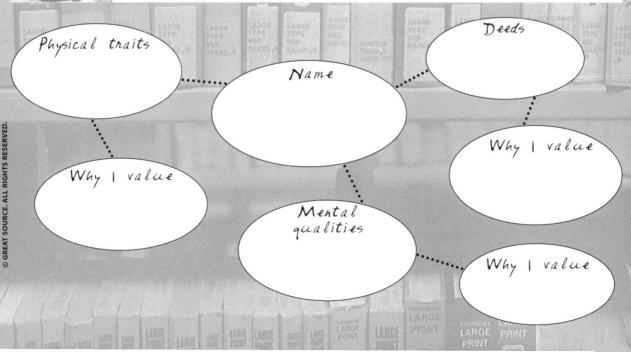

Physical traits

Deeds

Name

Why I value

Why I value

Mental qualities

Why I value

●✧ Write a tribute to your hero or heroine in the form of a poem or short essay. Study how Walker and Hayden constructed their tributes. Reveal not only the qualities of character you admire but why you value this person.

52

Often the heroes or heroines that you identify with are those that most nearly represent your own values and experiences.

New Ways of Seeing and Knowing

The phrase "new ways of seeing and knowing" may seem unusual. After all, if an object is in front of us, don't we know what we're looking at? Not always. If you have looked through a microscope, you know that there is more to a drop of water than what is visible to the naked eye. Or, depending on your previous experiences, a dog that looks friendly to you may look dangerous to a friend.

To some extent, the same ideas apply to reading. Closer examination often reveals more insights than an initial reading does. And, like the case of the friendly/dangerous dog, some of the meaning you take from a text depends on your previous experiences.

When you comprehend literally, you understand the details that are directly stated. Interpretive comprehension requires that you go beyond the details to understand the ideas that are implied. Critical comprehension requires that you apply or evaluate the details and ideas in the text. Active readers move among all three levels of comprehension.

One Seeing the Details

Paying attention to details is important for all levels of comprehension. Read the excerpt below from *Blue Highways: A Journey Into America* by William Least Heat Moon. He had lost his job teaching, was separated from his wife, and felt he had no direction in his life. He decided to travel around the country, following the "blue highways," back roads that are designated on maps by blue lines. In this excerpt, he has pulled off the road and is sitting by a spring. Trying to focus on his surroundings, he remembers something his father told him.

Response notes

from *Blue Highways: A Journey Into America*
William Least Heat Moon

It's a contention of Heat Moon's—believing as he does any traveler who misses the journey misses about all he's going to get—that a man becomes his attentions. His observations and curiosity, they make and remake him.

Etymology: *curious*, related to *cure*, once meant "carefully observant." Maybe a tonic of curiosity would counter my numbing sense that life inevitably creeps toward the absurd. *Absurd*, by the way, derives from a Latin word meaning "deaf, dulled." Maybe the road could provide a therapy through observation of the ordinary and obvious, a means whereby the outer eye opens an inner one. STOP, LOOK, LISTEN, the old railroad crossing signs warned. Whitman calls it "the profound lesson of reception."

New ways of seeing can disclose new things: the radio telescope revealed quasars and pulsars, and the scanning electron microscope showed the whiskers of the dust mite. But turn the question around: Do new *things* make for new ways of seeing?

In each box, jot down your ideas about what the phrases mean. Discuss them with others to see what other interpretations are possible.

PHRASE	PHRASE
a man becomes his attentions	Maybe the road could provide a therapy through observation of the ordinary and obvious
"the profound lesson of reception"	Do new things make for new ways of seeing?

In reading, as in traveling, it is important to pay attention to the details.

54

Two
Seeing the Literal Meaning

One way to understand the literal meaning of a text is to try to envision a scene. Use your "mind's eye" to picture the scene that Rachel Carson describes in this essay from her book *The Edge of the Sea*. Carson, a marine biologist, often wrote about the ocean and was well known for her concern for the environment.

from **"The Marginal World"** by Rachel Carson

The edge of the sea is a strange and beautiful place. All through the long history of Earth it has been an area of unrest where waves have broken heavily against the land, where the tides have pressed forward over the continents, receded, and then returned. For no two successive days is the shore line precisely the same. Not only do the tides advance and retreat in their eternal rhythms, but the level of the sea itself is never at rest. It rises or falls as the glaciers melt or grow, as the floor of the deep ocean basin shifts under its increasing load of sediments, or as the Earth's crust along the continental margins warps up or down in adjustment to strain and tension. Today a little more land may belong to the sea, tomorrow a little less. Always the edge of the sea remains an elusive and indefinable boundary.

The shore has a dual nature, changing with the swing of the tides, belonging now to the land, now to the sea. On the ebb tide it knows the harsh extremes of the land world, being exposed to heat and cold, to wind, to rain and drying sun. On the flood tide it is a water world, returning briefly to the relative stability of the open sea.

Only the most hardy and adaptable can survive in a region so mutable, yet the area between the tide lines is crowded with plants and animals. In this difficult world of the shore, life displays its enormous toughness and vitality by occupying almost every conceivable niche. Visibly, it carpets the intertidal rocks; or half hidden, it descends into fissures and crevices, or hides under boulders, or lurks in the wet gloom of sea caves. Invisibly, where the casual observer would say there is no life, it lies deep in the sand, in burrows and tubes and passageways. It tunnels into solid rock and bores into peat and clay. It encrusts weeds or drifting spars or the hard, chitinous shell of a lobster. It exists minutely, as the film of bacteria that spreads over a rock surface or a wharf piling; as spheres of protozoa, small as pinpricks, sparkling at the surface of the sea; and as Lilliputian beings swimming through dark pools that lie between the grains of sand.

The shore is an ancient world, for as long as there has been an earth and sea there has been this place of the meeting of land and water. Yet it is a world that keeps alive the sense of continuing creation and of the relentless drive of life. Each time that I enter it, I gain some new awareness of its beauty and its deeper meanings, sensing that intricate fabric of life by which one creature is linked with another, and each with its surroundings.

In my thoughts of the shore, one place stands apart for its revelation of exquisite beauty. It is a pool hidden within a cave that one can visit only rarely and briefly when the lowest of the year's low

← Response notes →

tides fall below it, and perhaps from that very fact it acquires some of
its special beauty. Choosing such a tide, I hoped for a glimpse of the
pool. The ebb was to fall early in the morning. I knew that if the wind
held from the northwest and no interfering swell ran in from a
distant storm the level of the sea should drop below the entrance to
the pool. There had been sudden ominous showers in the night, with
rain like handfuls of gravel flung on the roof. When I looked out into
the early morning the sky was full of a gray dawn light but the sun
had not yet risen. Water and air were pallid. Across the bay the moon
was a luminous disc in the western sky, suspended above the dim line
of distant shore—the full August moon, drawing the tide to the low,
low levels of the threshold of the alien sea world. As I watched, a gull
flew by, above the spruces. Its breast was rosy with the light of the
unrisen sun. The day was, after all, to be fair.

Later, as I stood above the tide near the entrance to the pool, the
promise of that rosy light was sustained. From the base of the steep
wall of rock on which I stood, a moss-covered ledge jutted seaward
into deep water. In the surge at the rim of the ledge the dark fronds
of oarweeds swayed, smooth and gleaming as leather. The projecting
ledge was the path to the small hidden cave and its pool. Occasionally
a swell, stronger than the rest, rolled smoothly over the rim and
broke in foam against the cliff. But the intervals between such swells
were long enough to admit me to the ledge and long enough for a
glimpse of that fairy pool, so seldom and so briefly exposed.

And so I knelt on the wet carpet of sea moss and looked back into
the dark cavern that held the pool in a shallow basin. The floor of the
cave was only a few inches below the roof, and a mirror had been
created in which all that grew on the ceiling was reflected in the still
water below.

Under water that was clear as glass the pool was carpeted with
green sponge. Gray patches of sea squirts glistened on the ceiling and
colonies of soft coral were a pale apricot color. In the moment when I
looked into the cave a little elfin starfish hung down, suspended by
the merest thread, perhaps by only a single tube foot. It reached down
to touch its own reflection, so perfectly delineated that there might
have been, not one starfish, but two. The beauty of the reflected
images and of the limpid pool itself was the poignant beauty of things
that are ephemeral, existing only until the sea should return to fill
the little cave.

Whenever I go down into this magical zone of the low water of the
spring tides, I look for the most delicately beautiful of all the shore's
inhabitants—flowers that are not plant but animal, blooming on the
threshold of the deeper sea. In that fairy cave I was not disappointed.
Hanging from its roof were the pendent flowers of the hydroid Tubularia,
pale pink, fringed and delicate as the wind flower. Here were
creatures so exquisitely fashioned that they seemed unreal, their
beauty too fragile to exist in a world of crushing force. Yet every
detail was functionally useful, every stalk and hydranth and petal-like
tentacle fashioned for dealing with the realities of existence. I knew
that they were merely waiting, in that moment of the tide's ebbing,

from **"The Marginal World"** by Rachel Carson

for the return of the sea. Then in the rush of water, in the surge of
surf and the pressure of the incoming tide, the delicate flower heads
would stir with life. They would sway on their slender stalks, and
their long tentacles would sweep the returning water, finding in it all
that they needed for life.

And so in that enchanted place on the threshold of the sea the
realities that possessed my mind were far from those of the land
world I had left an hour before.

←—*Response notes* —→

●◆ In the space below, sketch the important details of the pool within the cave as
they appear in your mind's eye. Don't worry about artistic ability. You are using
sketching as a thinking tool here, so feel free to make stick figures.

57

Using your mind's eye—
envisioning the scene an author
describes—as you read is a way to
improve your comprehension
of the details and the literal
meaning.

Observing and Interpreting

Writers carefully select the details that go into their finished works. For some writers, that requires precise observation to record a scene. Yet, the job of the writer just begins with recording details. The next step is to give those details meaning for the reader. Active readers read "between the lines" to interpret the meanings.

from **"Freedom and Wilderness"** by Edward Abbey

←— Response notes —→

Let me tell you a story.

A couple of years ago I had a job. I worked for an outfit called Defenders of Fur Bearers (now known as Defenders of Wildlife). I was caretaker and head janitor of a 70,000-acre wildlife refuge in the vicinity of Aravaipa Canyon in southern Arizona. The Whittell Wildlife Preserve, as we called it, was a refuge for mountain lion, javelina, a few black bear, maybe a wolf or two, a herd of whitetail deer, and me, to name the principal fur bearers.

I was walking along Aravaipa Creek one afternoon when I noticed fresh mountain lion tracks leading ahead of me. Big tracks, the biggest lion tracks I've seen anywhere. Now I've lived most of my life in the Southwest, but I am sorry to admit that I had never seen a mountain lion in the wild. Naturally I was eager to get a glimpse of this one.

It was getting late in the day, the sun already down beyond the canyon wall, so I hurried along, hoping I might catch up to the lion and get one good look at him before I had to turn back and head home. But no matter how fast I walked and then jogged along, I couldn't seem to get any closer; those big tracks kept leading ahead of me, looking not five minutes old, but always disappearing around the next turn in the canyon.

Twilight settled in, visibility getting poor. I realized I'd have to call it quits. I stopped for a while, staring upstream into the gloom of the canyon. I could see the buzzards settling down for the evening in their favorite dead cottonwood. I heard the poor-wills and the spotted toads beginning to sing, but of that mountain lion I could neither hear nor see any living trace.

I turned around and started home. I'd walked maybe a mile when I thought I heard something odd behind me. I stopped and looked back—nothing; nothing but the canyon, the running water, the trees, the rocks, the willow thickets. I went on and soon I heard that noise again—the sound of footsteps.

I stopped. The noise stopped. Feeling a bit uncomfortable now—it was getting dark—with all the ancient superstitions of the night starting to crawl from the crannies of my soul, I looked back again. And this time I saw him. About fifty yards behind me, poised on a sand bar, one front paw still lifted and waiting, stood this big cat, looking straight at me. I could see the gleam of the twilight in his eyes. I was startled as always by how small a cougar's head seems but how long and lean and powerful the body really is. To me, at that moment, he looked like the biggest cat in the world. He looked dangerous. Now I know very well that mountain lions are supposed

from **"Freedom and Wilderness"** by Edward Abbey

almost never to attack human beings. I knew there was nothing to fear—but I couldn't help thinking maybe this lion is different from the others. Maybe he knows we're in a wildlife preserve, where lions can get away with anything. I was not unarmed; I had my Swiss army knife in my pocket with the built-in can opener, the corkscrew, the two-inch folding blade, the screwdriver. Rationally there was nothing to fear; all the same I felt fear.

And something else too: I felt what I always feel when I meet a large animal face to face in the wild: I felt a kind of affection and the crazy desire to communicate, to make some kind of emotional, even physical contact with the animal. After we'd stared at each other for maybe five seconds—it seemed at the time like five minutes—I held out one hand and took a step toward the big cat and said something ridiculous like, "Here kitty, kitty." The cat paused there on three legs, one paw up as if he wanted to shake hands. But he didn't respond to my advance.

I took a second step toward the lion. Again the lion remained still, not moving a muscle, not blinking an eye. And I stopped and thought again and this time I understood that however the big cat might secretly feel, I myself was not yet quite ready to shake hands with a mountain lion. Maybe someday. But not yet. I retreated.

I turned and walked homeward again, pausing every few steps to look back over my shoulder. The cat had lowered his front paw but did not follow me. The last I saw of him, from the next bend of the canyon, he was still in the same place, watching me go. I hurried on through the evening, stopping now and then to look and listen, but if that cat followed me any further I could detect no sight or sound of it.

I haven't seen a mountain lion since that evening, but the experience remains shining in my memory. I want my children to have the opportunity for that kind of experience. I want my friends to have it. I want even our enemies to have it—they need it most. And someday, possibly, one of our children's children will discover how to get close enough to that mountain lion to shake paws with it, to embrace and caress it, maybe even teach it something, and to learn what the lion has to teach us.

59

●◆ What are your immediate reactions to this story? Write down what it makes you think about and your opinion of what Abbey says.

Abbey tells about conflicting feelings in this selection. He also leaves room for the reader to infer what he is feeling. Use the chart below to explore how his observations provoke particular feelings in him.

Abbey's Observations	Abbey's Reactions	My Interpretation
sees tracks	"eager to get a glimpse"	He's curious about seeing something he has not seen.

60

Look at your chart to complete this sentence:
Edward Abbey wants the reader to understand that

Four

Looking Beneath the Surface

What seems simple at the literal level may reveal complex meanings at the interpretive level. Reading can be like finding a geode. Geodes look like the other brownish-gray, rough rocks around them. But, when they're cut in half, they reveal uniquely beautiful arrangements of crystals. In the same way, active readers look beneath the surface to discover what the arrangement of ideas reveals.

Listen while someone reads aloud Sylvia Plath's "Mushrooms." Concentrate on the literal meaning as you listen.

Response notes

Mushrooms
Sylvia Plath

Overnight, very
Whitely, discreetly,
Very quietly

Our toes, our noses
Take hold on the loam,
Acquire the air.

Nobody sees us,
Stops us, betrays us;
The small grains make room.

Soft fists insist on
Heaving the needles,
The leafy bedding,

Even the paving.
Our hammers, our rams,
Earless and eyeless,

Perfectly voiceless,
Widen the crannies,
Shoulder through holes. We

Diet on water,
On crumbs of shadow,
Bland–mannered, asking

Little or nothing.
So many of us!
So many of us!

We are shelves, we are
Tables, we are meek,
are edible,

61

Nudgers and shovers ⟩
In spite of ourselves.
Our kind multiplies:

We shall by morning
Inherit the earth.
Our foot's in the door.

Plath gives the mushrooms attributes that we are more likely to use for people or common objects. For example, she says they are "nudgers and shovers" and calls them "shelves" and "tables." Go back through the poem and find five of these attributes. In the response notes, write down what qualities each attribute suggests. An example is next to "nudgers and shovers."

●◆ Demonstrate your understanding of the poem by writing an interpretive paragraph. Tell how a certain type of person or object is like the mushrooms.

62

Looking beneath the surface of a text will reveal additional insights and meanings.

Five

Comprehending Critically

Critical comprehension is often considered to be reading "behind the lines." You apply what you know by using information to express opinions and form new ideas. One way to apply what you know is to test the text against what you have learned from your own experiences.

One way to comprehend critically is to use information from the reading to express your opinion. Read an excerpt from near the end of *Blue Highways: A Journey Into America*. William Least Heat Moon is in Virginia, headed home in his van, Ghost Dancing, to Missouri.

from ***Blue Highways: A Journey Into America*** by William Least Heat Moon

When I saw Cuckoo, Virginia, it was a historical marker and a few houses at an intersection. I went up U.S. 33 until the rumple of hills became a long, bluish wall across the western sky. On the other side of Stanardsville in the Blue Ridge Mountains, I stopped in a glen and hiked along Swift Run, a fine rill of whirligigs and shiners, until I found a cool place for lunch. Summer was a few days away, but the heat wasn't.

Water striders and riffle bugs cut angles and arcs on smooth backwaters of the stream that reflected cirrus clouds crossing the ridges. They would make West Virginia before I did. I was sitting at the bottom of the eastern side of the Appalachians; when I came out of the mountains again, I would be in the Middle West. Sixteen dollars in my pocket. The journey was ending.

In a season on the blue roads, what had I accomplished? I hadn't sailed the Atlantic in a washtub, or crossed the Gobi by goat cart, or bicycled to Cape Horn. In my own country, I had gone out, had met, had shared. I had stood as witness.

I took a taste of Swift Run, went back to the highway, and followed it up Massanutten Mountain. Again the going was winding and slow. Near sunset, I reached West Virginia and drove on to Franklin, a main-street hamlet sharing a valley with a small river as the Appalachian towns do. Above the South Fork, above a hayfield, and under the mountains, I pulled in for the night.

After a small meal in the Ghost, I marked on a map the wandering circle of my journey. From the heartland out and around. A blue circle gone beyond itself. "Everything the Power of the World does is done in a circle," Black Elk says. "Even the seasons form a great circle in their changing, and always come back again to where they were. The life of a man is a circle from childhood to childhood, and so it is in everything where power moves."

Then I saw a design. There on the map, crudely, was the labyrinth of migration the old Hopis once cut in their desert stone. For me, the migration had been to places and moments of glimpsed clarity. Splendid gifts all.

← Response notes →

63

This is an account of the significance the journey had for him. Least Heat Moon writes things that are open to disagreement. For example, you may disagree with Black Elk that "The life of a man is a circle from childhood to childhood." Or you might disagree with, "so it is in everything where power moves." You also could disagree with Least Heat Moon about what he had accomplished by the journey.

✒ Express your opinion about one of the statements in the excerpt. Be sure to include reasons and examples for your opinion.

When you read, you apply the information and ideas of the author to what you already know.

Perspectives on a Subject: The Vietnam War

If you want to know what really happened after that controversial call at the game last weekend, what do you do? You could ask a friend. If you want to find out more, you could try the newspaper. You could even try to find out if the coach or a player knows a different version of the events.

Active readers and writers realize how important it is to explore a subject from several perspectives.

They know that any one story, poem, or memoir can present only part of the total picture. That is because writers must select a topic for their focus, rather than trying to cover everything at once. The topics they select and how fully they explore them depend on their audience and purpose.

Numerous articles, poems, books, and films have been written or made about the Vietnam War. This event from recent American history continues to concern millions of people. So much about the topic is still controversial that it serves as a good example of ways different perspectives can explore a subject.

One

Can you think of a time when you heard two or more conflicting stories about something that happened? How did you know what to believe? Why were the stories different from each other? The difference may be attributed to the self-interests of the person telling the story or how much that person actually saw. Active readers need to ask questions about the evidence provided and about the source.

A **fact** is something that can be proved true by consulting a reference or using firsthand observation. It is a fact that you are reading this paragraph. An **opinion** is someone's judgment or prediction and cannot be verified in the same ways as a fact. You are the only one who knows if this paragraph makes sense to you. However, opinions can be supported with facts, examples, quotations from experts, or other kinds of evidence. You will also find generalizations in your reading. A **generalization** is different from an opinion; it is a conclusion based on the available evidence. Supported generalizations include some or all of the evidence the writer used to reach a conclusion.

Read one account below of the history of the Vietnam War. Watch for facts and opinions and how they are supported.

from ***Voices from Vietnam*** by Barry Denenberg

←——*Response notes*——→

The Vietnamese have a long history, much of it spent fighting to remain independent of foreign conquerors. For centuries Vietnam was ruled by China. Then, in the mid-1800's, France seized control and made Vietnam one of its colonies. The French wanted to use Vietnam's raw materials and exploit the local population. Most Vietnamese, especially the peasants, suffered under French rule.

In 1945, after the end of World War II, Vietnamese resistance intensified and grew into a revolt, led by Ho Chi Minh, a Vietnamese communist. The French, however, did not take Ho Chi Minh's army seriously. They called it "the barefoot army." The French, well equipped and well trained, were able to control the cities. But "the barefoot army" was able to gain control of the countryside, where eighty-five percent of the population lived.

Back home, in France, the war had grown unpopular. It had dragged on longer than expected. The French called it "the dirty war." On May 7, 1954, the Vietnamese communists defeated the French in a decisive battle near the village of Dienbienphu, ending "the dirty war."

By that time American money had been paying for nearly eighty percent of the cost of the French war in Vietnam. Now, with France's defeat at Dienbienphu, the United States prepared to take its place.

Reread the excerpt and identify a statement that is an opinion. Then find a fact, quote, or example that supports it.

opinion:

support:

Now, read the next segment of Denenberg's history.

from *Voices from Vietnam* by Barry Denenberg

←—Response notes—→

President Dwight D. Eisenhower believed, as President Truman had before him, that Vietnam must not be allowed to become a communist country. Unless America maintained a powerful presence in the region, the Soviet Union and China could extend their influence throughout Southeast Asia. Eisenhower was determined not to let these small countries fall to the communists.

> You have a row of dominoes set up, and you knock over the first one and what will happen to the last one is the certainty that it will go over very quickly. So you have the beginning of a disintegration that will have the most profound influences.
> President Dwight D. Eisenhower

Two months after the fall of Dienbienphu, the Vietminh and the French signed a cease-fire agreement. The cease-fire was one of the provisions called for by an international conference held in Geneva, Switzerland. The conference had been called to solve cold war problems, including Vietnam. The United States, France, Great Britain, China, the Soviet Union, and representatives of North and South Vietnam were among the nine delegations attending the two-and-a-half-month-long meeting.

The delegates to Geneva recommended that nationwide elections be held in 1956 and that Vietnam be temporarily divided at the 17th parallel. The North would be ruled by Ho Chi Minh's communists and the South by the recently formed government of Ngo Dinh Diem.

President Eisenhower backed the anticommunist Diem and praised him as a "miracle man." The United States supported him with money and material.

> The Central Intelligence Agency was given the mission of helping Diem develop a government that would be sufficiently strong and viable to compete with and, if necessary, stand up to the Communist regime of Ho Chi Minh in the north.
> Chester Cooper, Central Intelligence Agency

67

What is your impression of the accuracy of this history so far? Does it seem to be true? Does Denenberg include enough believable evidence? Rate the accuracy of the excerpts on the scale below. Circle the number that best represents your rating.

1	2	3	4
Not Accurate			Very Accurate

●◆ Explain your rating of the selection. What supports your impressions?

....

....

....

A critical reader examines all of the evidence, carefully considering what are facts and what are opinions, before deciding what to believe.

If a writer wants to give an **objective** account of an event, he or she must present evidence from as many sides as possible. Here Barry Denenberg explains why the Americans made a mistake when they trusted Ngo Dinh Diem. As you read, consider the evidence he presents about Diem.

from ***Voices from Vietnam*** by Barry Denenberg

← Response notes →

Because of his privileged background, Diem had little sympathy for the common Vietnamese peasants who lived in the small villages and hamlets.

Soon after taking office Diem announced that he would not allow nationwide elections intended to unite the country to take place. His government, he said, was too new and therefore too weak. He ignored repeated requests from Ho Chi Minh that the elections be held.

Diem's government proved to be dictatorial, not democratic. He consolidated power in the hands of his family: three of his brothers held important positions in the government. The most powerful was his ruthless and corrupt brother Ngo Dinh Nhu. Nhu used a secret police force to repress any opposition. His wife, Madame Nhu, became an outspoken and controversial member of the government in her own right.

> (She) would tell American officers straight to their faces that her government did not like Americans but it liked having our money.
>   Jan Barry, U. S. Army

By 1958 there were 40,000 political prisoners in South Vietnamese jails. Twelve thousand others had been killed. New laws allowed military courts to execute anyone suspected of disloyalty to the Diem government within three days of their arrest. Mere suspicion was grounds for arrest, and there was no appealing the sentence.

Diem grew even more isolated from the people he was supposed to represent. He became increasingly unpopular as he continued to rule South Vietnam more like an emperor than a president.

> Though Diem had established his own patriotism in years past, he had never been actively engaged in the French war and had spent the last four years of it outside Vietnam. As a result, he viewed the resistance veterans as rivals for power who had to be crushed. Labeling all of them communists or pro-communist, he was using the secret police . . . to hunt down these people—people who were considered by almost everyone else as freedom fighters.
> Watching the political evolution of my country, I saw that the Diem government had many fundamental errors: First, it was a government of one family. Second, Diem suppressed many patriots who participated in the war against the French. Third, he put the Christian religion above the interest of the nation . . . eighty percent of the Vietnamese population are Confucian or Buddhists.
>   Truong Nhu Tang, Vietcong

68

How does this excerpt affect your view of this part of the background of the Vietnam War? Make a generalization about Denenberg's use of evidence and then support it with facts, examples, and quotations.

Firsthand Experience

Barry Denenberg uses an **objective** point of view to present the history of the Vietnam War. He does not appear to be personally involved in the story and gives the reader information from several different sources.

Another way to learn about a subject is to read the accounts of people who were involved. Firsthand accounts can be powerful, but must be read with an understanding of the author's subjective point of view. The author's emotional involvement in the event will certainly influence the selection of details and the presentation of events. Active readers understand that a **subjective** point of view offers insights into a subject that an objective point of view will not.

Consider this excerpt from Le Ly Hayslip's memoir *When Heaven and Earth Changed Places*. When she was twelve, the war came to her Vietnamese village of Ky La. From that time, the village was always occupied by one side or the other. She suffered rape, torture, hunger, and imprisonment. In 1970, she married an American soldier and came to the United States. The excerpt tells about how she felt when she saw the damage done to her people and culture by the war. Her father refers to her by her family nickname, Bay Ly.

← *Response notes* →

from ***When Heaven and Earth Changed Places*** by Le Ly Hayslip

I left my mother at sunrise praying for my safety. Both she and Ba had tried to discourage me from making the trip—saying there were rumors that my father had been beaten and that danger was everywhere—but they understood neither the risks I had taken in my business nor the fact that I knew Americans to be a bit less brutal and more trustworthy than either the Vietnamese or Viet Cong forces. To avoid combatants on either side, I traced the route I had taken in the storm almost three years before, through the swamps, jungle, hills, and brush country from Danang to Marble Mountains to Ky La but this time the weather was fine and I had plenty of time to think about my father and what to do when I got home. When I arrived, however, the village I remember no longer existed.

Half of Ky La had been leveled to give the Americans a better "killing zone" when defending the village. Their camp, which was a complex of bunkers and trenches with tin roofs, sandbags, radio antennas, and tents, lorded over the village from a hilltop outside of town. Around its slopes, homeless peasants and little kids poked through the American garbage in hopes of finding food or something to sell. In the distance, through a screen of withered trees (which had been defoliated now by chemicals as well as bombs), I could see that Bai Gian had not been rebuilt, and that the few remaining temples, pagodas, and wayside shrines—even my old schoolhouse and the guardsmen's awful prison—had been wiped away by the hand of war. Beautiful tropical forests had been turned into a bomb-cratered desert. It was as if the American giant, who had for so long been taunted and annoyed by the Viet Cong ants, had finally come to stamp its feet—to drive the painted, smiling Buddha from his house and substitute instead the khaki, glowering God of Abraham.

With the sickening feeling that I was now a stranger in my own homeland, I crossed the last few yards to my house with a lump in

from **When Heaven and Earth Changed Places** by Le Ly Hayslip

←—Response notes—→

my throat and a growing sense of dread. Houses could be rebuilt and damaged dikes repaired—but the loss of our temples and shrines meant the death of our culture itself. It meant that a generation of children would grow up without fathers to teach them about their ancestors or the rituals of worship. Families would lose records of their lineage and with them the umbilicals to the very root of our society—not just old buildings and books, but *people* who once lived and loved like them. Our ties to our past were being severed, setting us adrift on a sea of borrowed Western materialism, disrespect for the elderly, and selfishness. The war no longer seemed like a fight to see which view would prevail. Instead, it had become a fight to see just how much and how far the Vietnam of my ancestors would be transformed. It was as if I was standing by the cradle of a dying child and speculating with its aunts and uncles on what the doomed baby would have looked like had it grown up. By tugging on their baby so brutally, both parents had wound up killing it. Even worse, the war now attacked Mother Earth—the seedbed of us all. This, to me, was the highest crime—the frenzied suicide of cannibals. How shall one mourn a lifeless planet?

Inside, the neat, clean home of my childhood was a hovel. What few furnishings and tools were left after the battles had been looted or burned for fuel. Our household shrine, which always greeted new arrivals as the centerpiece of our family's pride, was in shambles. Immediately I saw the bag of bones and torn sinew that was my father lying on his bed. Our eyes met briefly but there was no sign of recognition in his dull face. Instead, he rolled away from me and asked:

"Where is your son?"

I crossed the room and knelt by his bed. I was afraid to touch him for fear of disturbing his wounds or tormenting his aching soul even more. He clutched his side as if his ribs hurt badly and I could see that his face was bruised and swollen.

"I am alone," I answered, swallowing back my tears. "Who did this to you?"

"Dich." (The enemy). It was a peasant's standard answer.

I went to the kitchen and made some tea from a few dried leaves. It was as if my father knew he was dying and did not wish the house or its stores to survive him. If one must die alone, it should be in an empty place without wasting a thing.

When I returned, he was on his back. I held his poor, scabbed head and helped him drink some tea. I could see he was dehydrated, being unable to draw water from the well or get up to drink it even when neighbors brought some to the house.

"Where were you taken? What was the charge?" I asked.

"It doesn't matter." My father drank gratefully and lay back on the bed. "The Americans came to examine our family bunker. Because it was so big, they thought Viet Cong might be hiding inside and ordered me to go in first. When I came out and told them no one was there, they didn't believe me and threw in some grenades. One of them didn't go off right away and the two Americans who went in

71

afterward were killed. They were just boys—" My father coughed up blood. "I don't blame them for being angry. That's what war is all about, isn't it? Bad luck. Bad karma."

"So they beat you up?"

"They pinned a paper on my back that said 'VC' and took me to Hoa Cam District for interrogation. I don't have to tell you what happened after that. I'm just lucky to be alive."

As sad as I felt about my father's misfortune, growing fury now burned inside me. There was no reason to beat this poor man almost to death because of a soldier's tragic mistake. . . .

I said I now regretted fleeing Ky La. Perhaps it would have been better to stay and fight—to fight the Americans with the Viet Cong or the Viet Cong with the Republicans or to fight both together by myself and with anyone else who would join me.

My father stopped eating and looked at me intently "Bay Ly, you were born to be a wife and mother, not a killer. That is your duty. For as long as you live, you must remember what I say. You and me—we weren't born to make enemies. Don't make vengeance your god, because such gods are satisfied only by human sacrifice."

"But there has been so much suffering—so much destruction!" I replied, again on the verge of tears, "Shouldn't someone be punished?"

"Are you so smart that you truly know who's to blame? If you ask the Viet Cong, they'll blame the Americans. If you ask the Americans, they'll blame the North. If you ask the North, they'll blame the South. If you ask the South, they'll blame the Viet Cong. If you ask the monks, they'll blame the Catholics, or tell you our ancestors did something terrible and so brought this endless suffering on our heads. So tell me, who would you punish? The common soldier on both sides who's only doing his duty? Would you ask the French or Americans to repay our Vietnamese debt?"

"But generals and politicians give orders—orders to kill and destroy. And our people cheat each other as if there's nothing to it. I know— I've seen it! And nobody has the right to destroy Mother Earth!"

"Well then, Bay Ly, go out and do the same, eh? Kill the killers and cheat the cheaters. That will certainly stop the war, won't it? Perhaps that's been our problem all along—not enough profiteers and soldiers!"

Despite my father's reasoning, my anger and confusion were so full-up that they burst forth, not with new arguments, but tears. He took me in his arms. "Shhh—listen, little peach blossom, when you see all those young Americans out there being killed and wounded in our war—in a war that fate or luck or god has commanded us to wage for our redemption and education—you must thank them, at least in your heart, for helping to put us back on our life's course. Don't worry about right or wrong. Those are weapons as deadly as bombs and bullets. Right is the goodness you carry in your heart—love for your ancestors and your baby and your family and for everything that lives. Wrong is anything that comes between you and that love. Go back to your little son. Raise him the best way you can. That is the battle you were born to fight. That is the victory you must win."

... the effects of the war? Describe them ... a paragraph.

... a third-person account like that of Denenberg and a first-person ... account like that of Hayslip.

Denenberg's Account	Hayslip's Account

●◆ Which account do you prefer? Why?

our Different Genres

What kind of information on a subject can you get from a poem? Poems do not present facts, at least in the way most people understand the word. So what value does a poem have in developing a subject? In his introduction to an anthology of poems about the Vietnam War, W. D. Ehrhart wrote, "Scholars and politicians, journalists and generals may argue, write and re-write 'the facts.' But when a poem is written, it becomes a singular entity with an inextinguishable and unalterable life of its own. It is a true reflection of the feelings and perceptions it records, and as such, it is as valuable a document as any history ever written."

Consider the feelings recorded in "The Next Step" by W. D. Ehrhart.

Response notes

The Next Step
W. D. Ehrhart

The next step you take
may lead you into an ambush.

The next step you take
may trigger a tripwire.

The next step you take
may detonate a mine.

The next step you take
may tear your leg off at the hip.

The next step you take
may split your belly open.

The next step you take
may send a sniper's bullet through your brain.

The next step you take.
The next step you take.

The next step.
The next step.

The next step.

74

●◇ Discuss the following questions with a partner. Then write your responses.

• What can you tell about the speaker? Male or female? Young or old?

• What "feelings and perceptions" does this poem "record"?

• How does the poet reinforce the feelings that a soldier would have?

75

• Why does Ehrhart include details that people might consider violent or gory?

• Why do you think the last stanza has only one line?

●◆ Write one or two paragraphs discussing Ehrhart's poem. Examine his emotions and feelings and what a poem can say that cannot be easily expressed in nonfiction.

A poem can provide a valuable perspective on a subject because its dense, reflective language can make a concise, yet potent, emotional statement.

Comparing Perspectives

There are many ways to learn about a topic and each way provides different information from a different **perspective**. Information may be presented from an **objective** or **subjective point of view** and may include **facts**, **opinions**, feelings, perceptions, and **generalizations**. Tim O'Brien wrote about the coverage of the Vietnam War: "It still boils down to suffering, and the thing about Vietnam that most bothers me is that it is treated as a political experience, a sociological experience, and the human element of what a soldier goes through—and what the Vietnamese went through—is not only neglected: it is almost cast aside as superfluous." What do you know now about both the politics and the human element of the war? Fill in the graphic with the information you received from each text.

Denenberg	Hayslip	Ehrhart

●◆ To see how changing your perspective can change your view of the subject, rewrite one of the three selections from a different point of view. For example, you could tell a segment of Hayslip's story from an objective angle or as a poem. Or write Ehrhart's poem as an objective report. Study the model for your piece carefully before you begin writing.

To understand a subject fully, it is important to examine it from many perspectives.

Shades of Meaning

Color pervades our language. When we are asked to describe something, we often begin with its color, then move on to size, shape, and other qualities. We can also describe language in terms of color. The color of language is its tone, mood, and voice. We need to look at the context of a word in order to understand its finer shades of meaning.

In a literal sense, we assume that what we see as the color red looks the same to everyone, when, in fact, that may not be true. The same thing is true of words in a figurative sense. Playing with the literal and figurative meanings is one of the ways that writers indulge their love of language. Writers explore the ways that shading can establish mood, lead to philosoph-

ical musings, or instill a desire to understand an aspect of nature.

Colors

My skin is kind of sort of brownish
Pinkish yellowish white
My eyes are greyish blueish green,
But I'm told they look orange in the night
My hair is reddish blondish brown,
But it's silver when it's wet
And all the colors I am inside
Haven't been invented yet.

Shel Silverstein

Shel Silverstein says it right: it's hard to define a particular color. A driver's license may say "eyes, brown," while the driver's eyes are a greyish bluish green. Even a color like black, which seems so solid, has many different hues. White, too, has many variations. Read Naomi Shihab Nye's poem "Defining White," noting your questions and ideas in the margin as you read.

Response notes

Defining White
Naomi Shihab Nye

On the telephone no one knows what white is.
My husband knows, he takes pictures.
He has whole notebooks defining
how white is white, is black,
and all the gray neighborhoods in between.

The telephone is blind.
Cream-white? Off-white?
I want a white, he says,
that is white-white,
that tends in no direction
other than itself.

Now this is getting complex.
Every white I see is tending
toward something else.
The house was white, but it is peeling.
People are none of these colors.

In the sky white sentences form and detach.
Who speaks here? What breath
scrawls itself endlessly,
white on white, without being heard?
Is wind a noun or a verb?

In column one of the double-entry log below, write three lines or sentences from the poem that make you stop and think. You might select sentences that you want to say more about, sentences that you find confusing, or just sentences that you like. In column two, write your own ideas about these lines from the poem.

lines from the poem	my ideas
"Is wind a noun or a verb?"	What does wind have to do with white? Does wind have a color? Or does it take the color of the air it passes through, like smoke or smog? It is a thing (noun) but it moves (verb).

●◆ "People are none of these colors," Nye wrote in line 16. What do "Defining White" and Shel Silverstein's poem "Colors" have in common?

●❖Nye writes, "Every white I see is tending / toward something else." In what way does the same thing happen with words? What do you think this means? Write a short essay explaining what you think it means and why it is, or is not, important.

Two Comparing to Define

There are many ways to define words. Defining **abstractions** like *democracy* or *freedom* is particularly difficult. But defining a color is a challenge, too, since what we think of as a color has to do with our own individual perception. You can do it directly or indirectly as Naomi Shihab Nye did in her poem "Defining White." Choose a color other than white. List everything you can think of that is some shade of the color you chose. Be sure you put concrete nouns here, things that have physical properties.

Pick three things from your list and describe the quality of your color for each object. Make your descriptions as specific as you can.

Objects from List	Description of the Quality of the Color
Example: computer paper	pure white, not creamy or grayish
1.	
2.	
3.	

Now take the three objects from your list and write two definitions for each. First, define your object using a **simile**—that is, a comparison using the word *like* or *as*. Then write a definition using a **metaphor**, an implied comparison. One example of each is given.

Objects	Definition of the Object's Color Using a Simile or Metaphor
Example: paper	Simile: The paper I am writing on is as white as new-fallen snow. Metaphor: The white paper blinds my eyes with its snowy brightness.
1.	Simile: Metaphor:
2.	Simile: Metaphor:
3.	Simile: Metaphor:

●◆ Using your descriptions and comparisons, write a poem defining the color you chose.

Defining words through similes and metaphors is one way to clarify the shades of meaning in your language.

Scientific and Poetic Language

Diane Ackerman explains why leaves turn color in the fall in the following passage. It gives an explanation for a commonly observed scientific phenomenon. Pay attention to her language as you read from *A Natural History of the Senses.*

from *A Natural History of the Senses* by Diane Ackerman

The stealth of autumn catches one unaware. Was that a goldfinch perching in the early September woods, or just the first turning leaf? A red-winged blackbird or a sugarmaple closing up shop for the winter? Keen-eyed as leopards, we stand still and squint hard, looking for signs of movement. Early-morning frost sits heavily on the grass, and turns barbed wire into a string of stars. On a distant hill, a small square of yellow appears to be a lighted stage. At last the truth dawns on us: Fall is staggering in, right on schedule, with its baggage of chilly nights, macabre holidays, and spectacular, heart-stoppingly beautiful leaves. Soon the leaves will start cringing on the trees, and roll up in clenched fists before they actually fall off. Dry seedpods will rattle like tiny gourds. But first there will be weeks of gushing color so bright, so pastel, so confettilike, that people will travel up and down the East Coast just to stare at it—a whole season of leaves.

Where do the colors come from? Sunlight rules most living things with its golden edicts. When the days begin to shorten, soon after the summer solstice on June 21, a tree reconsiders its leaves. All summer it feeds them so they can process sunlight, but in the dog days of summer the tree begins pulling nutrients back into its trunk and roots, pares down, and gradually chokes off its leaves. A corky layer of cells forms at the leaves' slender petioles, then scars over. Undernourished, the leaves stop producing the pigment chlorophyll, and photosynthesis ceases. Animals can migrate, hibernate, or store food to prepare for winter. But where can a tree go? It survives by dropping its leaves, and by the end of autumn only a few fragile threads of fluid-carrying xylem hold leaves to their stems.

A turning leaf stays partly green at first, then reveals splotches of yellow and red as the chlorophyll gradually breaks down. Dark green seems to stay longest in the veins, outlining and defining them. During the summer, chlorophyll dissolves in the heat and light, but it is also being steadily replaced. In the fall, on the other hand, no new pigment is produced, and so we notice the other colors that were always there, right in the leaf, although chlorophyll's shocking green hid them from view. With their camouflage gone, we see these colors for the first time all year, and marvel, but they were always there, hidden like a vivid secret beneath the hot glowing greens of summer.

←—*Response notes*—→

In some ways this passage sounds scientific. In others, it sounds poetic. Using the chart on the next page, note two passages (words, phrases or sentences) that fit into each of the two categories—scientific and poetic.

Passages that sound scientific	Passages that sound poetic

●◆ Explain why you selected these passages. What made a passage seem scientific or poetic?

●◆ How would you classify the writing of Diane Ackerman based on the sample you just read?

Platero and I is the most famous work of Juan Ramón Jiménez, a Nobel Prize-winning Spanish poet. The book is composed of short chapters describing life in and around a remote Spanish town, seen through the eyes of the author as he talks to his silver-gray donkey Platero. (*Plata* means "silver" in Spanish.) Read this passage to observe how richly Jiménez used color to convey his vision.

"Landscape in Scarlet" from *Platero and I*
Juan Ramón Jiménez

The hilltop. The setting sun lies pierced by his own crystal spears, bleeding purple and crimson from every vein. Before his splendor the green pine grove is dulled, turns vaguely red; and from the flushed transparent grass and small flowers a penetrating and luminous essence emanates.

I stop entranced in the twilight. Platero, his black eyes turned to scarlet by the sunset, walks softly to a pool of crimson, violet, rose-colored waters; gently he sinks his mouth in these mirrors, which again become liquid at his touch; and there is a profuse passing of dark waters up his huge throat.

I know this place well; but the moment has changed it and made it portentous. At any moment an unearthly adventure may befall us, an abandoned castle may loom before us. . . . . Evening prolongs itself beyond itself, and the hour, imbued with the spirit of eternity, is infinite, peaceful, beyond sounding.

"Come, Platero."

87

Mood is the feeling a piece of literature arouses in the reader. This describes the overall atmosphere a writer creates with language, imagery, descriptive details, and so on. Write a one-sentence description of what you think is the mood of Jiménez's piece. Then discuss your ideas as a class.

Identify several passages that you think are important in establishing the mood. Copy them in column one and analyze them to determine what creates mood. For example, is it the piling up of adjectives? the use of strong action words? the use of color words? Be as specific as you can.

Key passages that establish mood	Analysis of how the passages create mood
Example: The setting sun lies pierced by his own crystal spears....	The sun is personified. The phrase "pierced by his own crystal spears" is vivid, visual. By turning the rays of the sun inward, the scene becomes bizarre, unreal.

●◆Using images from the chapter, sketch symbols or scenes that depict the mood or tone of this passage. Title your drawing with a word that describes the mood.

Title:

Good readers often focus on the mood of a piece of literature because it helps them understand their reaction to it.

Five

Visualizing Words

Throughout the centuries, rainbows have been **symbols** of vision and hope. A Greek myth tells of Iris, messenger of the gods, who traveled the path of the rainbow to bring messages to people on the earth. In the rainbow, we have all colors, the full spectrum that we are able to perceive as our eyes move from red to orange to yellow to green to blue to indigo and finally violet. In the poem "Visions," Joy Harjo shows us another view of the rainbow.

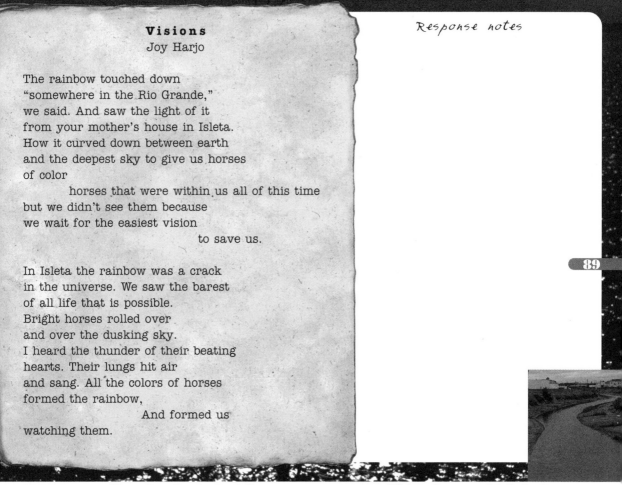

Visions
Joy Harjo

The rainbow touched down
"somewhere in the Rio Grande,"
we said. And saw the light of it
from your mother's house in Isleta.
How it curved down between earth
and the deepest sky to give us horses
of color
        horses that were within us all of this time
but we didn't see them because
we wait for the easiest vision
                to save us.

In Isleta the rainbow was a crack
in the universe. We saw the barest
of all life that is possible.
Bright horses rolled over
and over the dusking sky.
I heard the thunder of their beating
hearts. Their lungs hit air
and sang. All the colors of horses
formed the rainbow,
                And formed us
watching them.

Response notes

89

Examine closely the following two quotations. Write what you think the lines mean.

Quotations

... horses that were within us all of this time
but we didn't see them because
we wait for the easiest vision
                to save us.

... All the colors of horses
formed the rainbow,
                And formed us
watching them.

My interpretation of these lines

●◆ Notice that Harjo writes an entire poem based on the colors of the rainbow, yet she never names a specific color. Did this affect your visualizing of the poem? Did you see it in color? Did you see all the colors of the rainbow? Would it have been more or less effective if she had used the names of the colors? Write a description of how you visualized this poem as you were reading. What were the most important visual words?

Writers help us see
the pictures in their writing
either by using direct description
or by using symbols that allow us
to visualize the specifics.

Words in Context

Reading is the best way there is to increase your vocabulary. Good readers know how to figure out the meaning of a passage even if it has unfamiliar words in it. They use the context of the whole passage to give them clues. Building a vocabulary is more than learning lists of words; it is also becoming aware of how even a familiar word may change meaning in different contexts.

Writing that deals with food is a good place to look at how words work. All kinds of writers write about food. Cookbooks are best-sellers; diet books abound; fast food addicts and natural food devotees find themselves the subjects of political columns, at odds politically as well as nutritionally. The school lunch menu is a topic of discussion in school newspapers across the country.

Whatever their intent, writers who write about food use words in a consciously specific way. They seem to care about words as much as they care about food.

One Sensory Language

In this passage from James Agee's *Let Us Now Praise Famous Men*, food is described to give us the flavor not only of biscuits and bacon, but of all the feelings and tastes of the home the narrator has long since left. As you read, let your senses experience the scene.

← *Response notes* →

from *Let Us Now Praise Famous Men* by James Agee

The biscuits are large and shapeless, not cut round, and are pale, not tanned, and are dusty with flour. They taste of flour and soda and damp salt and fill the mouth stickily. They are better with butter, and still better with butter and jam. The butter is pallid, soft, and unsalted, about the texture of cold-cream; it seems to taste delicately of wood and wet cloth; and it tastes "weak." The jam is loose, of little berries, full of light raspings of the tongue; it tastes a deep sweet purple tepidly watered, with a very faint sheen of a sourness as of iron. Field peas are olive-brown, the shape of lentils, about twice the size. Their taste is a cross between lentils and boiled beans; their broth is bright with seasoning of pork, and of this also they taste. The broth is soaked up in bread. The meat is a bacon, granular with salt, soaked in the grease of its frying: there is very little lean meat in it. What there is is nearly as tough as rind; the rest is pure salted stringy fat. The eggs taste of pork too. They are fried in it on both sides until none of the broken yolk runs, are heavy salted and peppered while they fry, so that they come to table nearly black, very heavy, rinded with crispness, nearly as dense as steaks. Of milk I hardly know how to say; it is skimmed, blue-lighted; to a city palate its warmth and odor are somehow dirty and at the same time vital, a little as if one were drinking blood. There is even in so clean a household as this an odor of pork, of sweat, so subtle it seems to get into the very metal of the cooking-pans beyond any removal of scrubbing, and to sweat itself out of newly washed cups; it is all over the house and all through your skin and clothing at all times, yet as you bring each piece of food to your mouth it is so much more noticeable, if you are not used to it, that a quiet little fight takes place on your palate and in the pit of your stomach; and it seems to be this odor, and a sort of wateriness and discouraged tepidity, which combine to make the food seem unclean, sticky, and sallow with some invisible sort of disease, yet this is the odor and consistency and temper and these are true tastes of home; I know this even of myself; and much as my reflexes are twitching in refusal of each mouthful a true homesick and simple fondness for it has so strong a hold of me that in fact there is no fight to speak of and no faking of enjoyment at all.

Reread the passage looking for any words whose meanings you don't know or are not sure of. Underline them and jot down your guesses about their meanings in the response notes.

Writers involve us in their worlds by using words that appeal to our senses. Which senses does Agee appeal to? Fill in the chart showing words and phrases from Agee's memoir that appeal to these senses. (Some columns may be blank.)

Sight	Sound	Taste	Smell	Touch

→ Write a paragraph about a particular food. Use as many of Agee's words as you can—both the unfamiliar words and the sensory words—to describe this food. Underline all of the words that you used from your Agee lists.

93

Being aware of how a writer uses sensory details enables you to understand a scene more fully.

Ways

Go back to the Agee text and look at the words you underlined. List these words in the left column of the chart below. In the next two columns, write what you think of as the usual meaning. Then write what the word seems to mean in this passage.

Word	Usual meaning	Apparent meaning in this passage

●◆ Imagine that you are revisiting a memorable meal. Make notes or a cluster showing how the food at this meal appealed to your senses and your emotions.

●◆ Describe this meal in a way that conveys its sensory and emotional appeal. Try to use some familiar words in unfamiliar ways.

Three

Words and Social History

M. F. K. Fisher has been described as a "discriminating gourmet and an observer of life." More important, she was a superb writer. Her subject, on the surface, is food. Unknowing people may refer to her as "the food writer." But, as you will see, she is much more than that.

In an early work, *Serve It Forth*, Fisher chronicled the way foods reveal the culture of a people. Here is what she says about the ancient Egyptians. Underline and make notations about the meaning of any words you find interesting, unusual, or unknown.

from *Serve It Forth* by M. F. K. Fisher

← *Response notes* →

In Egypt they ate quite simply. Every-day bread was made from *spelt*, the dried pounded centers of the sacred lotus plants, and for feasts fine wheaten flour in loaves. They caught fish and spread them in the sun to dry, thick with salt.

All the Egyptians ate leeks and onions with some impunity, but tried to hide their passion for garlic from the priests, who most fastidiously denounced it as an unclean abomination.

Ox meat was roasted or boiled, but many kinds of little birds, and even quails and ducks, were salted and eaten raw. And melons in increasing variety made fine the poorest fare, with grapes and figs and dates, and barley beer, and sweet wine in great pottery vases glazed with blue.

Honey from the richly flowered delta had already in those far days been changed into a hundred kinds of sweetmeats, or baked into the breads, or simmered with the flesh of melons and fruits to make the same heavy voluptuous confitures that travellers eat today in Alexandria.

Then, as now, the Egyptians were temperate and frugal, but always hospitable. They welcomed strangers as well as kin to their meals, where men and women ate together, and where, for the most part, the lowest *fellahin* and members of the royal family ate much the same simple food.

It was in the tools for eating, and the dining-rooms, that caste difference most clearly showed itself. The peasants and the artisans used pottery, glazed blue or red, perhaps, but always simple, and they sat on benches in their low mud houses.

The palaces of the wealthy people, the nobles and scientists, were airy and beautiful, surrounded by pools and arboured gardens, and built with carved painted columns to hold the canopies that made their walls.

Everywhere, on the stone pillars and the embroidered linens, and in the faience, and the gold that was "plentiful as dust," the sacred lotus and the date frond curved and lifted.

At feasts guests sat upon wooden armchairs, heavily inlaid with gold and stones, and made more comfortable by soft cushions of leather and silky Egyptian linen. They ate from delicate spoons of

95

←—Response notes—→ carved wood or ivory, and drank from lotus-cups of blue glaze or, later, of iridescent glass. Bowls, no matter how simple their contents, were of the common gold, or rarer silver, or the most valuable bronze.

Unlike the Greeks and Romans, who barred women from all banqueting, and only invited the hetaerae to come in with the final wines for philosophic dalliance, the Egyptians dined easily together. While the lords and ladies tarried over their cool courses of melons and sweet wine, dancers entertained them with slow gay rhythms, or more highly educated singers, usually women, chanted to the ancient plaintive sounds of lutes and pipes.

●◆ Select three of the words you underlined. Describe why you underlined them and then explain what these words convey about the Egyptian culture.

Word	why I selected this word
1:	
2:	
3:	

What these words convey about ancient Egyptian culture:

●◆ Think about the different cultures that you and your classmates represent. Select one group that has a definable culture (style of dress, language, eating habits) and describe the group's food habits. What do these reveal about the world of the members?

97

Focusing on the language writers use to describe a culture enables you to understand its distinctiveness.

Simple Words, Complex Ideas

Some of the most profound or complex ideas may be expressed in simple, everyday language. In this piece by Margaret Atwood, the idea of bread is presented in several different scenarios. The first time through, read to get a sense of the whole.

"Bread" by Margaret Atwood

←—*Response notes*—→

Imagine a piece of bread. You don't have to imagine it, it's right here in the kitchen, on the breadboard, in its plastic bag, lying beside the bread knife. The bread knife is an old one you picked up at an auction; it has the word BREAD carved into the wooden handle. You open the bag, pull back the wrapper, cut yourself a slice. You put butter on it, then peanut butter, then honey, and you fold it over. Some of the honey runs out onto your fingers and you lick it off. It takes you about a minute to eat the bread. This bread happens to be brown, but there is also white bread, in the refrigerator, and a heel of rye you got last week, round as a full stomach then, now going moldy. Occasionally you make bread. You think of it as something relaxing to do with your hands.

Imagine a famine. Now imagine a piece of bread. Both of these things are real but you happen to be in the same room with only one of them. Put yourself into a different room, that's what the mind is for. You are now lying on a thin mattress in a hot room. The walls are made of dried earth, and your sister, who is younger than you, is in the room with you. She is starving, her belly is bloated, flies land on her eyes; you brush them off with your hand. You have a cloth too, filthy but damp, and you press it to her lips and forehead. The piece of bread is the bread you've been saving, for days it seems. You are as hungry as she is, but not yet as weak. How long does this take? When will someone come with more bread? You think of going out to see if you might find something that could be eaten, but outside the streets are infested with scavengers and the stink of corpses is everywhere.

Should you share the bread or give the whole piece to your sister? Should you eat the piece of bread yourself? After all, you have a better chance of living, you're stronger. How long does it take to decide?

Imagine a prison. There is something you know that you have not yet told. Those in control of the prison know that you know. So do those not in control. If you tell, thirty or forty or a hundred of your friends, your comrades, will be caught and will die. If you refuse to tell, tonight will be like last night. They always choose the night. You don't think about the night however, but about the piece of bread they offered you. How long does it take? The piece of bread was brown and fresh and reminded you of sunlight falling across a wooden floor. It reminded you of a bowl, a yellow bowl that was once in your home. It held apples and pears; it stood on a table you can also remember. It's not the hunger or the pain that is killing you but the absence of the yellow bowl. If you could only hold the bowl in your hands, right here, you could withstand anything, you tell yourself. The bread they

"Bread" by Margaret Atwood

←—Response notes—→

offered you is subversive, it's treacherous, it does not mean life.

There were once two sisters. One was rich and had no children, the other had five children and was a widow, so poor that she no longer had any food left. She went to her sister and asked her for a mouthful of bread. "My children are dying," she said. The rich sister said, "I do not have enough for myself," and drove her away from the door. Then the husband of the rich sister came home and wanted to cut himself a piece of bread, but when he made the first cut, out flowed red blood.

Everyone knew what that meant.

This is a traditional German fairy tale.

The loaf of bread I have conjured for you floats about a foot above your kitchen table. The table is normal, there are no trap doors in it. A blue tea towel floats beneath the bread, and there are no strings attaching the cloth to the bread or the bread to the ceiling or the table to the cloth, you've proved it by passing your hand above and below. You didn't touch the bread though. What stopped you? You don't want to know whether the bread is real or whether it's just a hallucination I've somehow duped you into seeing. There's no doubt that you can see the bread, you can even smell it, it smells like yeast, and it looks solid enough, solid as your own arm. But can you trust it? Can you eat it? You don't want to know, imagine that.

99

●◆ Use the following space to draw a symbol for each of the five sections of the piece. Title each section.

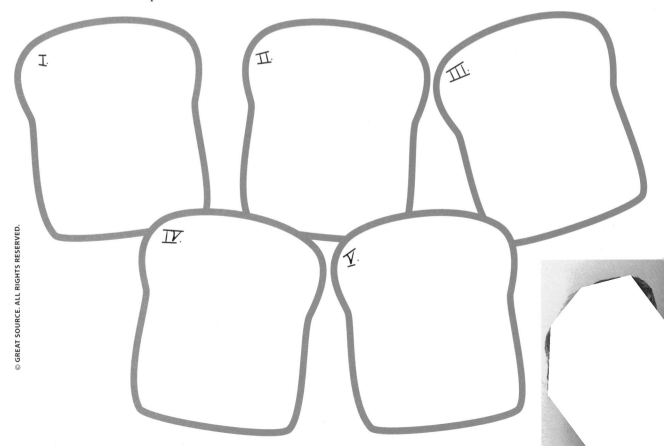

I.

II.

III.

IV.

V.

➡️ Now look at Atwood's use of language. Note that her words are primarily simple, everyday words. If you find any unusual words, or unusual uses of words, list them here with your comments.

➡️ Write your ideas about the meaning of this piece. Address such questions as what puzzles you about it, what image or images stand out for you, and what feelings it evokes.

100

One of the ways that Atwood achieves her effect of immediacy in her piece is her use of the present tense. Rewrite the following part of the first paragraph in the past tense and see how that changes the effect:

> The bread knife is an old one you picked up at an auction; it has the word BREAD carved into the wooden handle. You open the bag, pull back the wrapper, cut yourself a slice. You put butter on it, then peanut butter, then honey, and you fold it over. Some of the honey runs out onto your fingers and you lick it off. It takes you about a minute to eat the bread.

●◆ Your revision, written in the past tense:

....

....

....

....

....

....

●◆ Discuss the following ideas with a classmate or small group:

1. How does the change of tense affect your feelings about this section?

....

....

....

2. Notice that one section is already written in the past tense. Why do you think this particular section is written this way?

....

....

....

3. When Atwood writes "Imagine a piece of bread," she is ordering us to enter into her scenarios. How effective is this as a strategy?

....

....

●◆ Write a prose piece modeled on Atwood's essay using another familiar concrete object instead of bread. Keep your language simple, using mostly nouns and verbs. Write it completely in the present tense. Begin with the word *imagine*.

Writers create powerful effects when they use such strategies as addressing the reader and writing in the present tense.

Focus on the Writer: John Steinbeck

John Steinbeck, one of the most widely read authors in the United States, was more than a novelist; he was also a social historian. Through his stories and novels, he focused attention on the troubles of ordinary people struggling to survive: itinerant farm laborers, immigrants from Mexico, Midwestern farmers beset by the Dustbowl of the 1930s, and others.

Through all of his works, Steinbeck remained true to his belief in what he called "the perfectibility of man," the idea that we can all make a difference in this world. He believed deeply that literature should try to make people's lives better.

Steinbeck was a champion of the oppressed and the outcasts of society. He extolled the simple joys of life, while exposing the unintended cruelties in society. He developed characters that remain with us long after the book is closed, and he vividly portrayed the Monterey region of California, an area he called "Las Pasturas del Cielo," the Pastures of Heaven.

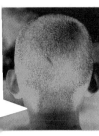

One The Unfinished Children of Nature

Steinbeck's characters are often confronted by their differences from other people. Many times they are simple-minded or even severely disabled, the people Steinbeck called the "unfinished children of nature." In *The Pastures of Heaven*, he tells stories of a number of people whose differences made them outcasts in their towns. One of the most poignant is the story of Tularecito, a child found "in the sagebrush beside the road." His name came from his appearance, which was that of a *tularecito*, or little frog. While his body grew and became extraordinarily strong, "after the fifth year his brain did not grow any more." When he was finally forced by law to go to school, his teacher discovered that although he could not learn, he could draw. However, he could not tolerate the destruction of his work. Read this account of what happened in his one-room school.

from ***The Pastures of Heaven*** by John Steinbeck

←—Response notes—→

When Miss Martin, the teacher, discovered his ability, she gave him a piece of chalk and told him to make a procession of animals around the blackboard. Tularecito worked long after school was dismissed, and the next morning an astounding parade was shown on the walls. All of the animals Tularecito had ever seen were there; all the birds of the hills flew above them. A rattlesnake crawled behind a cow; a coyote, his brush proudly aloft, sniffed at the heels of a pig. There were tomcats and goats, turtles and gophers, every one of them drawn with astonishing detail and veracity.

Miss Martin was overcome with the genius of Tularecito. She praised him before the class and gave a short lecture about each one of the creatures he had drawn. In her own mind she considered the glory that would come to her for discovering and fostering this genius.

"I can make lots more," Tularecito informed her.

Miss Martin patted his broad shoulder. "So you shall," she said. "You shall draw every day. It is a great gift that God has given you." Then she realized the importance of what she had just said. She leaned over and looked searchingly into his hard eyes while she repeated slowly, "It is a great gift that God has given you." Miss Martin glanced up at the clock and announced crisply, "Fourth grade arithmetic at the board."

The fourth grade struggled out, seized erasers and began to remove the animals to make room for their numbers. They had not made two sweeps when Tularecito charged. It was a great day. Miss Martin, aided by the whole school, could not hold him down, for the enraged Tularecito had the strength of a man, and a madman at that. The ensuing battle wrecked the schoolroom, tipped over the desks, spilled rivers of ink, hurled bouquets of teacher's flowers about the room. Miss Martin's clothes were torn to streamers, and the big boys, on whom the burden of the battle fell, were bruised and battered cruelly. Tularecito fought with hands, feet, teeth and head. He admitted no honorable rules and in the end he won. The whole school, with Miss Martin guarding its rear, fled from the building, leaving the enraged Tularecito in possession. When they were gone, he locked the door, wiped the blood out of his eyes and set to work to repair the animals that had been destroyed.

●◆ On the basis of this much of the story, make a prediction about what you think might happen to Tularecito.

Miss Martin leaves at the end of the school year, unable to deal with Tularecito. She is replaced by Miss Morgan, who gives Tularecito his own space to draw above the chalkboards. During one of her daily readings to her students, Tularecito becomes entranced with the story of gnomes, strange creatures with whom he identifies. In his search, at night, for these elusive creatures, Tularecito digs a deep hole to wait for them. When the local farmer comes upon the hole and tries to fill it in, Tularecito, predictably, becomes enraged again. After the locals finally subdue him, they take him to jail. Later, the judge says to Frank Gomez, the man who found him as a child and has been his protector, "You must see that we cannot let him go loose. Sooner or later he will succeed in killing someone." After a short deliberation, the judge committed Tularecito to the asylum for the criminal insane at Napa.

Discuss with a partner or group how your predictions of what happened to Tularecito compared to Steinbeck's ending of the story.

●◆ How did what happened to Tularecito make you feel?

What has Steinbeck done to evoke your feelings about Tularecito? Select examples to show how the descriptive passages, the action, and the dialogue contribute to your response. Use the chart below.

Categories	Passage from Text	What this passage made me think or feel about Tularecito
Descriptive passage		
Action		
Dialogue		

Description, action, and dialogue all contribute to the development of a believable character.

Two
Character Relationships

There is a character similar to Tularecito in one of Steinbeck's most famous novels, *Cannery Row*. The **setting** is the Western Biological, a lab run by Doc, the main character of the novel. In this scene, we are introduced to Frankie. As you read, make notations that give you insight into both characters, Doc and Frankie. (Notes: Purple Velella are small, brilliantly colored marine animals that look as though they have wings. They are sometimes called "flying sailors." *Excelsior* refers to a loosely shredded packing material that was widely used before the invention of plastic.)

from *Cannery Row* by John Steinbeck

←—Response notes—→

Frankie began coming to Western Biological when he was eleven years old. For a week or so he just stood outside the basement door and looked in. Then one day he stood inside the door. Ten days later he was in the basement. He had very large eyes and his hair was a dark wiry dirty shock. His hands were filthy. He picked up a piece of excelsior and put it in a garbage can and then he looked at Doc where he worked labeling specimen bottles containing purple Velella. Finally Frankie got to the work bench and he put his dirty fingers on the bench. It took Frankie three weeks to get that far and he was ready to bolt every instant of the time.

Finally one day Doc spoke to him. "What's your name, son?"

"Frankie."

"Where do you live?"

"Up there," a gesture up the hill.

"Why aren't you in school?"

"I don't go to school."

"Why not?"

"They don't want me there."

"Your hands are dirty. Don't you ever wash?"

Frankie looked stricken and then he went to the sink and scrubbed his hands and always afterwards he scrubbed his hands almost raw every day.

And he came to the laboratory every day. It was an association without much talk. Doc by a telephone call established that what Frankie said was true. They didn't want him in school. He couldn't learn and there was something a little wrong with his co-ordination. There was no place for him. He wasn't an idiot, he wasn't dangerous, his parents, or parent, would not pay for his keep in an institution. Frankie didn't often sleep at the laboratory but he spent his days there. And sometimes he crawled in the excelsior crate and slept. That was probably when there was a crisis at home.

Doc asked, "Why do you come here?"

"You don't hit me or give me a nickel," said Frankie.

"Do they hit you at home?"

"There's uncles around all the time at home. Some of them hit me

107

and tell me to get out and some of them give me a nickel and tell me
to get out."
    "Where's your father?"
    "Dead," said Frankie vaguely.

●◆ Why do you think Doc lets Frankie spend so much time in the laboratory?

....

....

....

....

    Later in the book, when Frankie has gained more confidence, he helps Doc not
only in the laboratory but also at the parties that Doc has there. Frankie is
overcome with pleasure because Doc had said to one of the guests that "Frankie is a
great help to me." Frankie dreams of a plan to show Doc how helpful he really can
be. On the night of a big party, he prepares a tray of filled glasses and takes the
heavy tray into the party. This is how the ending of the chapter reads. Again, make
notes about what happens.

    Now he was ready. He took a great breath and opened the door.
The music and the talk roared around him. Frankie picked up the tray
of beer and walked through the door. He knew how. He went straight
toward the same young woman who had thanked him before. And
then right in front of her, the thing happened, the co-ordination failed,
the hands fumbled, the panicked muscles, the nerves telegraphed to a
dead operator, the responses did not come back. Tray and beer
collapsed forward into the young woman's lap. For a moment Frankie
stood still. And then he turned and ran.
    The room was quiet. They could hear him run downstairs and go
into the cellar. They heard a hollow scrabbling sound and then silence.
Doc walked quietly down the stairs and into the cellar. Frankie was in
the excelsior box burrowed down clear to the bottom, with the pile of
excelsior on top of him. Doc could hear him whimpering there. Doc
waited for a moment and then he went quietly back upstairs.
    There wasn't a thing in the world he could do.

●◆ Do you agree that "There wasn't a thing in the world he could do"? Write your ideas and explain what this scene tells you about Doc and his relationship with Frankie.

The Unfinished Child as an Adult

There are many memorable characters in Steinbeck's novels, but the ones that readers probably recognize more than any others are George and Lennie from *Of Mice and Men*. They are itinerant farmhands. George describes their lives: "Guys like us, that work on ranches, are the loneliest guys in the world. They got no family. They don't belong no place." George tries to protect Lennie, "the imbecile giant who out of tenderness alone squeezes the life out of every living creature that comes into his hands." But George cannot be around twenty-four hours a day.

Read this excerpt from *Of Mice and Men*. As you read, record your ideas and feelings about the character Lennie.

from ***Of Mice and Men*** by John Steinbeck

←─ *Response notes* ─→

Only Lennie was in the barn, and Lennie sat in the hay beside a packing case under a manger in the end of the barn that had not been filled with hay. Lennie sat in the hay and looked at a little dead puppy that lay in front of him. Lennie looked at it for a long time, and then he put out his huge hand and stroked it, stroked it clear from one end to the other.

And Lennie said softly to the puppy, "Why do you got to get killed? You ain't so little as mice. I didn't bounce you hard." He bent the pup's head up and looked in its face, and he said to it, "Now maybe George ain't gonna let me tend no rabbits, if he fin's out you got killed."

He scooped a little hollow and laid the puppy in it and covered it over with hay, out of sight; but he continued to stare at the mound he had made. He said, "This ain't no bad thing like I got to go hide in the brush. Oh! no. This ain't. I'll tell George I foun' it dead."

He unburied the puppy and inspected it, and he stroked it from ears to tail. He went on sorrowfully, "But he'll know. George always knows. He'll say, 'You done it. Don't try to put nothing over on me.' An' he'll say, 'Now jus' for that you don't get to tend no rabbits!'"

In the space below, sketch Lennie as you see or think of him. You may draw a realistic picture or let a key image symbolize Lennie.

In *Of Mice and Men*, we are reading about a severely retarded grown man, one of Steinbeck's "unfinished children of nature," being looked after by an itinerant farmhand who has no other family. As you did with Tularecito, find places in the text where Steinbeck develops the character of Lennie with description, action, or dialogue. Then describe what each of these selections tells you about Lennie.

Categories	Passages in the text	What the passage tells about Lennie
Description		
Action		
Dialogue		

●◆ Describe how Steinbeck makes us feel Lennie's remorse. What passages in the text reflect this remorse?

While readers learn about characters through straightforward description and actions, they must also look carefully at the thoughts of the characters themselves.

In *The Grapes of Wrath*, Steinbeck created the famous characters of the Joad family who travel across the country after losing their farm in Oklahoma. Like the countless people who actually made this journey in the 1930s, the Joads confront the realities of an America divided into those with land and money and those without. Steinbeck himself made such a journey with a family like the Joads as he was preparing to write about this difficult time for many people.

In the following scene, set in Oklahoma, Tom has returned home from prison to find his family loading their old truck to go to California. After greeting his father outside, he goes in to surprise his mother, who is cooking breakfast and doesn't recognize his silhouette in the doorway. Pa had yelled to her to expect another person for breakfast.

← *Response notes* →

from *The Grapes of Wrath* by John Steinbeck

Tom stood looking in. Ma was heavy, but not fat; thick with child-bearing and work. She wore a loose Mother Hubbard of gray cloth in which there had once been colored flowers, but the color was washed out now, so that the small flowered pattern was only a little lighter gray than the background. The dress came down to her ankles, and her strong, broad, bare feet moved quickly and deftly over the floor. Her thin, steel-gray hair was gathered in a sparse wispy knot at the back of her head. Strong, freckled arms were bare to the elbow, and her hands were chubby and delicate, like those of a plump little girl. She looked out into the sunshine. Her full face was not soft; it was controlled, kindly. Her hazel eyes seemed to have experienced all possible tragedy and to have mounted pain and suffering like steps into a high calm and a superhuman understanding. She seemed to know, to accept, to welcome her position, the citadel of the family, the strong place that could not be taken. And since old Tom and the children could not know hurt or fear unless she acknowledged hurt and fear, she had practiced denying them in herself. And since, when a joyful thing happened, they looked to see whether joy was on her, it was her habit to build up laughter out of inadequate materials. But better than joy was calm. Imperturbability could be depended upon. And from her great and humble position in the family she had taken dignity and a clean calm beauty. From her position as healer, her hands had grown sure and cool and quiet; and faultless in judgment as a goddess. She seemed to know that if she swayed the family shook, and if she ever really deeply wavered or despaired the family would fall, the family will to function would be gone.

She looked out into the sunny yard, at the dark figure of a man. Pa stood near by, shaking with excitement. "Come in," he cried. "Come right in, mister." And Tom a little shamefacedly stepped over the doorsill.

She looked up pleasantly from the frying pan. And then her hand sank slowly to her side and the fork clattered to the wooden floor. Her

from **The Grapes of Wrath** by John Steinbeck

eyes opened wide, and the pupils dilated. She breathed heavily, through her open mouth. She closed her eyes. "Thank God," she said. "Oh, thank God!" and suddenly her face was worried. "Tommy, you ain't wanted? You didn' bust loose?"

"No, Ma. Parole. I got the papers here." He touched his breast.

She moved toward him lithely, soundlessly in her bare feet, and her face was full of wonder. Her small hand felt his arm, felt the soundness of his muscles. And then her fingers went up to his cheek as a blind man's fingers might. And her joy was nearly like sorrow. Tom pulled his underlip between his teeth and bit it. Her eyes went wonderingly to his bitten lip, and she saw the little line of blood against his teeth and the trickle of blood down his lip. Then she knew, and her control came back, and her hand dropped. Her breath came out explosively. "Well!" she cried. "We come mighty near to goin' without ya. An' we was wonderin' how in the worl' you could ever find us." She picked up the fork and combed the boiling grease and brought out a dark curl of crisp pork. And she set the pot of tumbling coffee on the back of the stove.

Steinbeck draws characters partially by direct description, partially by how other characters view them or think of them, and partially by their actions. Reread the passage and select key words and phrases to fill out the chart below.

Response notes

113

Direct description of Ma	What we know of Ma from Tom's thoughts or actions	What we know of Ma from her actions

Steinbeck also tells us a lot about his characters by what they don't do. Find a moment in the passage when Ma or Tom do not do what you might have expected them to do.

Passage when Ma or Tom do not do what I might have expected	How do I account for the way they behave toward each other in this passage?

●◆ During the moment when Ma and Tom face each other, Steinbeck wrote, "Then she knew." Based on your analysis of her character in this scene, what do you think he meant by that sentence? Go back to your notes and charts before you write your response to this question.

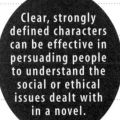

Clear, strongly defined characters can be effective in persuading people to understand the social or ethical issues dealt with in a novel.

Five

The Perfectibility of Man

When Steinbeck was awarded the Nobel Prize in Literature in 1962, he was cited "for his realistic as well as imaginative writing, distinguished by a sympathetic humor and a keen social perception." This prize is the highest honor for a writer, acknowledging a lifetime of literary achievement. Here is an excerpt from Steinbeck's Nobel Prize lecture.

---

from **The Nobel Prize Lecture** by John Steinbeck

←—Response notes—→

Literature is as old as speech. It grew out of human need for it and it has not changed except to become more needed. The skalds, the bards, the writers are not separate and exclusive. From the beginning, their functions, their duties, their responsibilities have been decreed by our species.

Humanity has been passing through a gray and desolate time of confusion. My great predecessor, William Faulkner, speaking here, referred to it as a tragedy of universal physical fear, so long sustained that there were no longer problems of the spirit, so that only the human heart in conflict with itself seemed worth writing about. Faulkner, more than most men, was aware of human strength as well as of human weakness. He knew that the understanding and the resolution of fear are a part of the writer's reason for being.

This is not new. The ancient commission of the writer has not changed. He is charged with exposing our many grievous faults and failures, with dredging up to the light or dark and dangerous dreams for the purpose of improvement.

Furthermore, the writer is delegated to declare and to celebrate man's proven capacity for greatness of heart and spirit—for gallantry in defeat, for courage, compassion and love. In the endless war against weakness and despair, these are the bright rally flags of hope and emulation. I hold that a writer who does not passionately believe in the perfectibility of man has no dedication nor any membership in literature.

115

●◆ Think about your own ideas about the role of the writer in society. Explain your views on this subject. Use quotations from Steinbeck's speech that you agree or disagree with to make your points.

One of Steinbeck's most passionate beliefs was in the "perfectibility of man." Look back over the excerpts from Steinbeck's works that you have read and see what correlations, if any, you can find between his writings and this idea. Find three quotations that refer to this idea and explain them in the chart below.

	Quotation	Meaning
1.		
2.		
3.		

●◆ Using the information from your chart, write about how Steinbeck presented his belief in the "perfectibility of man" in his novels.

Knowing what a writer believes in can help in understanding his or her characters and stories.

Essentials of Reading

The poet Louise Glück wrote, "Major experiences vary in form— what reader and writer learn to do is recognize analogies." This is what we do when we read, but how do we go about reading and making the right analogies?

What are some essentials of reading? What aspects of a text should a reader spend the most time on? How can you be sure that you truly understand what a story or poem or essay is about?

Active readers know that they need to be able to think along with the writer. They need to understand the author's theme, be able to read between the lines, and somehow get hold of the author's intent or purpose in writing. In the lessons that follow, you'll examine these and other essentials of reading.

Whether we're aware of it or not, we are constantly making predictions as we read. If we read a novel, we predict how it will end; if we read a love story, we make predictions about whether the lovers will marry. We combine what we already know with the author's words to make sense of what we read.

As you read Kate Chopin's "The Story of an Hour," stop to make a few predictions about character and plot. Each time you make a prediction, take a moment to jot down some notes about why you think your prediction will happen.

"The Story of an Hour" by Kate Chopin

← Response notes →

Knowing that Mrs. Mallard was afflicted with a heart trouble, great care was taken to break to her as gently as possible the news of her husband's death.

It was her sister Josephine who told her, in broken sentences; veiled hints that revealed in half concealing. Her husband's friend Richards was there, too, near her. It was he who had been in the newspaper office when intelligence of the railroad disaster was received, with Brently Mallard's name leading the list of "killed." He had only taken the time to assure himself of its truth by a second telegram, and had hastened to forestall any less careful, less tender friend in bearing the sad message.

She did not hear the story as many women have heard the same, with a paralyzed inability to accept its significance. She wept at once, with sudden, wild abandonment, in her sister's arms. When the storm of grief had spent itself she went to her room alone. She would have no one follow her.

There stood, facing the open window, a comfortable, roomy armchair. Into this she sank, pressed down by a physical exhaustion that haunted her body and seemed to reach into her soul.

STOP AND PREDICT

What do you think Mrs. Mallard will do now that she is alone in her room?

She could see in the open square before her house the tops of trees   ←─Response notes─→
that were all aquiver with the new spring life. The delicious breath of
rain was in the air. In the street below a peddler was crying his wares.
The notes of a distant song which someone was singing reached her
faintly, and countless sparrows were twittering in the eaves.

There were patches of blue sky showing here and there through
the clouds that had met and piled one above the other in the west
facing her window.

She sat with her head thrown back upon the cushion of the chair,
quite motionless, except when a sob came up into her throat and
shook her, as a child who has cried itself to sleep continues to sob in
its dreams.

She was young, with a fair, calm face, whose lines bespoke
repression and even a certain strength. But now there was a dull
stare in her eyes, whose gaze was fixed away off yonder on one of
those patches of blue sky. It was not a glance of reflection, but rather
indicated a suspension of intelligent thought.

There was something coming to her and she was waiting for it,
fearfully. What was it? She did not know; it was too subtle and
elusive to name. But she felt it, creeping out of the sky, reaching
toward her through the sounds, the scents, the color that filled the air.

Now her bosom rose and fell tumultuously. She was beginning to
recognize this thing that was approaching to possess her, and she was
striving to beat it back with her will—as powerless as her two white
slender hands would have been.

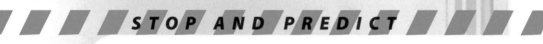

STOP AND PREDICT

●❖ Will she be able to conquer this thing?

....

....

....

When she abandoned herself a little whispered word escaped her   ←─Response notes─→
slightly parted lips. She said it over and over under her breath: "free,
free, free!" The vacant stare and the look of terror that had followed
it went from her eyes. They stayed keen and bright. Her pulses beat
fast, and the coursing blood warmed and relaxed every inch of her
body.

She did not stop to ask if it were or were not a monstrous joy that
held her. A clear and exalted perception enabled her to dismiss the
suggestion as trivial.

She knew that she would weep again when she saw the kind,
tender hands folded in death; the face that had never looked save
with love upon her, fixed and gray and dead. But she saw beyond that
bitter moment a long procession of years to come that would belong to
her absolutely. And she opened and spread her arms out to them in
welcome.

119

"The Story of an Hour" by Kate Chopin

There would be no one to live for her during those coming years; she would live for herself. There would be no powerful will bending hers in that blind persistence with which men and women believe they have a right to impose a private will upon a fellow-creature. A kind intention or a cruel intention made the act seem no less a crime as she looked upon it in that brief moment of illumination.

And yet she loved him—sometimes. Often she had not. What did it matter! What could love, the unsolved mystery, count for in the face of this possession of self-assertion which she suddenly recognized as the strongest impulse of her being!

"Free! Body and soul free!" she kept whispering.

Josephine was kneeling before the closed door with her lips to the keyhole, imploring for admission. "Louise, open the door! I beg; open the door—you will make yourself ill. What are you doing, Louise? For heaven's sake open the door."

"Go away. I am not making myself ill." No; she was drinking in a very elixir of life through that open window.

Her fancy was running riot along those days ahead of her. Spring days, and summer days, and all sorts of days that would be her own. She breathed a quick prayer that life might be long. It was only yesterday she had thought with a shudder that life might be long.

She arose at length and opened the door to her sister's importunities. There was a feverish triumph in her eyes, and she carried herself unwittingly like a goddess of Victory. She clasped her sister's waist, and together they descended the stairs. Richards stood waiting for them at the bottom.

Someone was opening the front door with a latchkey. It was Brently Mallard who entered, a little travel-stained, composedly carrying his gripsack and umbrella. He had been far from the scene of accident, and did not even know there had been one. He stood amazed at Josephine's piercing cry; at Richards' quick motion to screen him from the view of his wife.

120

STOP AND PREDICT

What do you think will happen when Louise sees her husband alive?

....

....

....

But Richards was too late.

When the doctors came they said she had died of heart disease—of joy that kills.

Now that you've finished reading "The Story of an Hour," you know whether or not your predictions came true. Predict what will happen in the hour after Louise's death. Use the chart on the next page to record your ideas.

	Louise falls dead.	The doctors announce Louise died of "joy."	After the doctors leave.
Josephine's reaction when . . .			
Brently's reaction when . . .			

→ Now use your chart to write a short narrative in which you describe the hour immediately following Louise's death. Use Chopin's style as a model for your own writing.

Active readers make predictions as they read. Most of the predictions are about what will happen or what characters are like.

Considering the Theme

Discovering the **theme** of a piece of writing is another reading essential. Sometimes an author will state the theme directly. More often the reader will have to infer the theme by looking carefully at what the author says and how he or she says it. In **fiction**, the theme can usually be found by taking a careful look at the characters and **plot** and what the author has to say about them.

In "The Story of an Hour," Chopin never makes a direct statement of the theme, though she clearly has one. Read the story again, this time keeping an eye out for the theme. Use the margins of the text for your notes. Discuss the story and its theme with another student. Try to answer the following questions together.

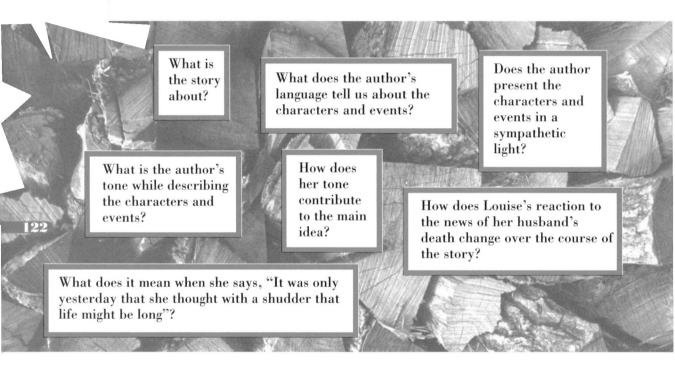

What is the story about?

What does the author's language tell us about the characters and events?

Does the author present the characters and events in a sympathetic light?

What is the author's tone while describing the characters and events?

How does her tone contribute to the main idea?

How does Louise's reaction to the news of her husband's death change over the course of the story?

What does it mean when she says, "It was only yesterday that she thought with a shudder that life might be long"?

122

●❖ Now explain Chopin's theme in your own words. Use quotations from the story to support your interpretation.

....

....

....

....

....

· Critical readers know that finding the theme is an essential part of reading. In fiction, character and plot descriptions can provide valuable clues about the theme.

Reading Between the Lines

Critical readers know that it is important to make inferences about what an author is saying—to read between the lines. These **inferences** can concern **characters**, **plot**, **theme**, **setting**, or any other element of the work. Let's say, for example, that a writer opens a story by describing a man walking alone on a highway at night. The man has a small pack slung over his shoulder and a hat pulled down low over his eyes. What inferences can you make about what you've read? You might logically infer that this is a man who doesn't want to be noticed (an inference about character) and that he is either walking away from or walking toward some kind of trouble (an inference about plot). You also might infer that the action takes place in a quiet, relatively unpopulated area (an inference about setting).

As you read an excerpt from Jane Smiley's Pulitzer Prize-winning novel *A Thousand Acres*, keep track of your inferences by jotting them down in the response notes.

from ***A Thousand Acres*** by Jane Smiley

← Response notes →

123

At sixty miles per hour, you could pass our farm in a minute, on County Road 686, which ran due north into the T intersection at Cabot Street Road. Cabot Street Road was really just another country blacktop, except that five miles west it ran into and out of the town of Cabot. On the western edge of Cabot, it became Zebulon County Scenic Highway, and ran for three miles along the curve of the Zebulon River, before the river turned south and the Scenic continued west into Pike. The T intersection of CR 686 perched on a little rise, a rise nearly as imperceptible as the bump in the center of an inexpensive plate.

From that bump, the earth was unquestionably flat, the sky unquestionably domed, and it seemed to me when I was a child in school, learning about Columbus, that in spite of what my teacher said, ancient cultures might have been on to something. No globe or map fully convinced me that Zebulon County was not the center of the universe. Certainly, Zebulon County, where the earth *was* flat, was one spot where a sphere (a seed, a rubber ball, a ballbearing) must come to a perfect rest and once at rest must send a taproot downward into the ten-foot-thick topsoil.

Because the intersection was on this tiny rise, you could see our buildings, a mile distant, at the southern edge of the farm. A mile to the east, you could see three silos that marked the northeastern corner, and if you raked your gaze from the silos to the house and barn, then back again, you would take in the immensity of the piece of land my father owned, six hundred forty acres, a whole section, paid for, no encumbrances, as flat and fertile, black, friable, and exposed as any piece of land on the face of the earth.

If you looked west from the intersection, you saw no sign of anything remotely scenic in the distance. That was because the Zebulon River had cut down through topsoil and limestone, and made its pretty course a valley below the level of the surrounding farmlands. Nor, except at night, did you see any sign of Cabot. You saw only this, two sets of farm buildings surrounded by fields. In the nearer set lived the Ericsons, who had daughters the ages of my sister Rose and myself, and in the farther set lived the Clarks, whose sons, Loren and Jess, were in grammar school when we where in junior high. Harold Clark was my father's best friend. He had five hundred acres and no mortgage. The Ericsons had three hundred seventy acres and a mortgage.

Acreage and financing were facts as basic as name and gender in Zebulon County. Harold Clark and my father used to argue at our kitchen table about who should get the Ericson land when they finally lost their mortgage. I was aware of this whenever I played with Ruthie Ericson, whenever my mother, my sister Rose, and I went over to help can garden produce, whenever Mrs. Ericson brought over some pies or doughnuts, whenever my father loaned Mr. Ericson a tool, whenever we ate Sunday dinner in the Ericsons' kitchen. I recognized the justice of Harold Clark's opinion that the Ericson land was on his side of the road, but even so, I thought it should be us. For one thing, Dinah Ericson's bedroom had a window seat in the closet that I coveted. For another, I thought it appropriate and desirable that the great circle of the flat earth spreading out from the T intersection of County Road 686 and Cabot Street Road be ours. A thousand acres. It was that simple.

It was 1951 and I was eight when I saw the farm and the future in this way. That was the year my father bought his first car, a Buick sedan with prickly gray velvet seats, so rounded and slick that it was easy to slide off the backseat into the footwell when we went over a stiff bump or around a sharp corner. That was also the year my sister Caroline was born, which was undoubtedly the reason my father bought the car. The Ericson children and the Clark children continued to ride in the back of the farm pickup, but the Cook children kicked their toes against a front seat and stared out the back windows, nicely protected from the dust. The car was the exact measure of six hundred forty acres compared to three hundred or five hundred. In spite of the price of gasoline, we took a lot of rides that year, something farmers rarely do, and my father never again did after Caroline was born. For me, it was a pleasure like a secret hoard of coins—Rose, whom I adored, sitting against me in the hot musty velvet luxury of the car's interior, the click of the gravel on its undercarriage, the sensation of the car swimming in the rutted road, the farms passing every minute, reduced from vastness to insignificance by our speed; the unaccustomed sense of leisure; most important, though, the reassuring note of my father's and mother's voices commenting on what they saw—he on the progress of the yearly work and the condition of the animals in the pastures, she on the look and size of the house and garden, the colors of the buildings. Their tones of voice were unhurried and self-confident, complacent with the knowledge that the work at our place was farther along, the buildings at our place more imposing and better cared for. When I

from **A Thousand Acres** by Jane Smiley

think of them now, I think how they had probably seen nearly as
little of the world as I had by that time. But when I listened to their
duet then, I nestled into the certainty of the way, through the
repeated comparisons, our farm and our lives seemed secure and
good.

←—Response notes—→

What inferences can you make about Smiley's characters, plot, and setting?
For example, what can you infer about the **narrator**? Is she an adult of the
1990s or an eight-year-old living on a farm in 1951? Use the chart below to
categorize some other inferences about character, plot, and setting.

Inferences about character	Inferences about plot	Inferences about setting
The narrator is an adult telling a story of her youth.	Smiley's action unfolds slowly.	The story takes place in the Midwest— Indiana or Iowa perhaps.

125

●◆ Based on what you know and what you can infer, write a short introduction to
this excerpt. Your introduction should offer readers information about the
characters, plot, and setting. Be sure to make your information as interesting as
possible so that a reader wants to read the selection.

It is important to
make inferences about what the
author is saying. These inferences
will improve your understanding of
a work's characters, plot, and
setting.

It is essential to understand exactly what you have read. An important part of understanding a work is rereading. You may need to read a selection two or even three times before the elements begin to come into focus. On a second reading, you are no longer worrying about what might happen and can focus on other aspects of the text. For example, on a second reading you can spend time thinking about elements such as the author's **style**, **point of view**, and **tone**.

Reread the excerpt from *A Thousand Acres*. **Annotate** the text by underlining words or passages that reflect Smiley's writing style, language, and tone. Then answer the questions.

●◆ Describe Smiley's writing style.

●◆ What are your impressions of Smiley's language? Does it strike you as simple? sophisticated? Does she use figurative language? If so, where?

◆◆ How would you describe Smiley's tone? What does her tone reveal about the narrator? What does it reveal about the setting?

Five Author's Purpose

Sometimes an author will make a direct statement of purpose: "I am writing this because I want to talk about television. . . ." More often, an author will only hint at his or her purpose for writing. It's up to the reader to infer the author's intent.

Readers can make **inferences** about the author's intent by examining the **form**, **style**, and **tone** of the writing. Each of these elements will provide valuable clues about the author's purpose. As you read Steve Wulf's *Time* magazine column, "A Flower in the Outfield," make some notes about Wulf's intent.

"A Flower in the Outfield" by Steve Wulf

We were yellow. We were sponsored by a garbage company. We were hit by pleurisy, near mutiny, vacations, brain cramps and pretty much every other squad in the league. Yet, when we see major leaguers celebrating in the upcoming postseason, we will remember how we felt back in June.

Let's see, we had Brady Anderson in center, Alex Rodriguez at short, Frank Thomas at first, Mike Piazza behind the plate, Jay Buhner in right, Ken Caminiti at third, Craig Biggio at second, Barry Bonds in left and Roger Clemens on the mound. Despite the presence of such stars, we lost our first six games—not counting a tie called for darkness. Actually, it was in an effort to lighten things up that the coaches decided to give our Little Leaguers the names of big leaguers with the corresponding positions, if not quite the talents.

Several of our players did share a trait with a Hall of Famer who once lived in our neighborhood: Lou Gehrig. It wasn't Larrupin' Lou's power, unfortunately, nor the longevity of the Iron Horse. Rather, it was the sensitivity of the young Gehrig, who would sit on the Yankee bench and cry if he didn't drive in an expected run. We led the league in tears if nothing else.

The first tears belonged to the two coaches, who were dealt the bad hand of yellow-and-white uniforms. The outfits for all the good teams in our league had handsome, powerful colors. No major league team wears yellow. When we took the field we looked like nine dandelions. We thought we had drafted a pretty good team. But it took us a while to get the talents in synch. Too many vacations, too little practice time, too many boneheaded plays, dropped fly balls and rotten coaching decisions. We improved noticeably toward the end of the season, but still. . . .

One thing was clear from the outset. This was the nicest group of kids either one of us had ever coached. This was also the most spirited group. We rallied from nine runs down against the best team in the league to send the game into extra innings. We ended up losing that game, and some other heartbreakers, but the players never gave

← Response notes →

127

"A Flower in the Outfield" by Steve Wulf

up. In one epic struggle late in the season, the umpire had to tell our players, who were at the fence cheering for their mate at bat, to sit down and be quiet.

While the players never gave us an ounce of sass or trouble, the season was not without incident. We had one zealous father who thought we weren't doing right by his son, and indeed we may have given the lad short shrift in response to being pressured. After a game in which I screwed up a substitution, which resulted in this player not getting an at-bat, the father somewhat publicly berated me and my coaching. But he was just a father who cared a lot about his son, and his son was a very sweet kid. Not to mention a pretty good hitter once we started giving him a few more at-bats.

We finished the regular season at 6–12. That meant we were seeded No. 11 in the 16-team, everybody-makes-it playoffs, pairing us off with the No. 6 seed. In the top of the first, we scored three runs with no outs when the son of the zealous dad hit a bases-clearing triple. We never scored another run after that. But lo and behold, our pitchers held the other team in check, thanks to some spectacular plays in the field. With two outs in the sixth, and last, inning, they had runners on first and second, while we had two outs and a 3–1 lead.

At which point, a routine fly ball was hit to our rightfielder, who had pitched two terrific innings earlier in the game. He dropped it. Now the score was 3–2, and there were runners on second and third. When I looked to the rightfielder, I saw him standing there, yellow hat in hand, glove between his legs, bawling.

I called time out and trotted out to the rightfield foul line. I tried as best I could to calm the rightfielder down, telling him that we were still winning, that we wouldn't be winning without him, that we needed him to put the glove back on. I also told him, though I'm not sure he heard me, not to worry about crying because Lou Gehrig cried.

The next batter up hit a long fly to right centerfield. I thought for sure it was going to fall in for the game-winning hit. But wait. Intersecting with the ball was a flash of yellow—our rightfielder. He caught it. He held onto it. In the next moment, he was engulfed in the outfield by his teammates.

As the lowest seed to advance to the next round of the playoffs, we had to play the No. 1 seed. We actually gave them a scare, rallying twice to keep the score close, but alas, our season ended in the second round.

Winning one inconsequential playoff game in one of thousands of Little Leagues can't compare with winning the World Series. Or can it? For Alex, Ari, Billy, Bo, Chaz, Frankie, Jeff, Jon, Joe, Mark, Sam and Zach, it can. One big yellow flower bloomed in the outfield that day. Daisy? Daffodil? It certainly wasn't a dandelion. Let's hope it's a perennial, even if only in their memory.

Take a moment to think about Wulf's essay. How does the presentation of his ideas reveal something of his purpose?

●◆ Describe how he structures the essay and the effect the dramatization has on you as a reader.

....

....

....

....

....

●◆ Describe Wulf's attitude toward the subject. What does this tell you about his purpose?

....

....

....

....

....

....

●◆ Who do you think is Wulf's intended audience and how does this relate to his purpose?

....

....

....

....

....

....

Share
your responses with a
partner and discuss how
these elements help
reveal purpose.

●◆ Write a letter to the editor in which you critique Wulf's column. Be sure to discuss what you think was Wulf's intention in writing the piece.

Understanding an author's purpose or intent is an essential part of reading. Many times the organization, style, and tone of a piece can provide clues to the author's intent.

131

Stories Through the Ages

Stories preserve the knowledge, values, history, and hopes of cultures and help to pass them from generation to generation.

There are 30,000-year-old paintings of animals on the walls of a cavern at Lascaux in France, and various speculations have been offered as to the purpose of the paintings. Some say the animal figures were drawn to honor the actual animals so they might flourish on earth. Other experts suggest that the pictures were used as part of a ritual to enact a successful hunt or to educate young boys about the hunt. Whatever the purpose of the drawings, it's likely that stories were told to accompany these images of the hunt, the tribe, and its gods.

Imagine being in the cave at night, shadows from a fire playing across the walls and the paintings shrouded in the haze of smoke that animates them. The voice of a storyteller echoes throughout the cavern. In such a setting, the first stories were told. They were probably explanations of human action interpreted through animal instinct and behavior.

Lessons in Animal Fables

Animal **fables** are some of the earliest and most enduring stories that link human experience to the natural world. Many of these stories come to us from the **oral tradition**. Fables are stories intended to teach a lesson. Generally the characters are animals who speak and act like people, and the animals' behavior is a mirror to human experience. A story about how a squirrel stores acorns for the winter reminds us that foresight is an important quality. The point is emphasized more dramatically if the story also has a chipmunk who goes hungry in the winter because he sleeps all day in the fall. As you read the following fable from India, notice the lesson taught by the monkey and the crocodile.

"The Monkey and the Crocodile" (Indian Folk Tale)

←—Response notes—→

A Monkey lived in a great tree on the riverbank. In the river there were many Crocodiles.

A Crocodile watched the Monkeys for a long time, and one day she said to her son: "My son, get one of those Monkeys for me. I want the heart of a Monkey to eat."

"How am I to catch a Monkey?" asked the little Crocodile. "I do not travel on land, and the Monkey does not go into the water."

"Put your wits to work, and you'll find a way," said the mother.

And the little Crocodile thought and thought.

At last he said to himself: "I know what I'll do. I'll get that Monkey that lives in a big tree on the riverbank. He wishes to go across the river to the island where the fruit is so ripe.

So the Crocodile swam to the tree where the Monkey lived. But he was a stupid Crocodile.

"Oh, Monkey," he said, "come with me over to the island where the fruit is so ripe."

"How can I go with you?" asked the Monkey. "I do not swim."

"No—but I do. I will take you over on my back," said the Crocodile. The Monkey was greedy, and wanted the ripe fruit, so he jumped down on the Crocodile's back.

"Off we go!" said the Crocodile.

"This is a fine ride you are giving me!" said the Monkey.

"Do you think so? Well, how do you like this?" asked the Crocodile, diving.

"Oh, don't!" cried the Monkey, as he went under the water. He was afraid to let go, and he did not know what to do under the water.

When the Crocodile came up, the Monkey sputtered and choked. "Why did you take me under water, Crocodile?" he asked.

"I am going to kill you by keeping you under water," answered the Crocodile. "My mother wants Monkey heart to eat, and I'm going to take yours to her."

"I wish you had told me you wanted my heart," said the Monkey, "then I might have brought it with me."

"How queer!" said the stupid Crocodile. "Do you mean to say that you left your heart back there in the tree?"

132

"The Monkey and the Crocodile" (Indian Folk Tale)

"That is what I mean," said the Monkey. "If you want my heart, we must go back to the tree and get it. But we are so near the island where the ripe fruit is, please take me there first."

"No, Monkey," said the Crocodile, "I'll take you straight back to your tree. Never mind the ripe fruit. Get your heart and bring it to me at once. Then we'll see about going to the island."

"Very well," said the Monkey.

But no sooner had he jumped onto the bank of the river than—whisk! up he ran into the tree.

From the topmost branches he called down to the Crocodile in the water below:

"My heart is way up here! If you want it, come for it, come for it!"

What characteristics of both the Crocodile and the Monkey can you relate to human behavior and intellect? List these qualities in the left column on the chart below. In the right column, explain what lessons people can learn from each animal.

characteristics	lessons

●◆ Write a paragraph that explains what you think is the general lesson of the story. Be sure to support your explanation with evidence from the story.

Fables
are stories
that teach
lessons about
human
concerns,
traits, and
actions.

Two

Fables in Cultural Context

The animal stories told in each culture reflect the unique circumstances of the group who is telling them. Many of the traditional stories from African American folklore have animals as central characters. Through the animals' actions and experiences, readers can gain insights into the questions and concerns of African Americans. The following tale was recorded by Zora Neale Hurston in the early 1930s as part of her research study on black folklore. It is included in her book *Mules and Men*.

The Hawk and the Buzzard (African American Folk Tale)
collected by Zora Neale Hurston

←—Response notes—→

You know de hawk and de buzzard was settin' up in a pine tree one day, so de hawk says: "How you get yo' livin', Brer Buzzard?"

"Oh Ah'm makin' out pretty good, Brer Hawk. Ah waits on de salvation of de Lawd."

Hawk says, "Humph, Ah don't wait on de mercy of nobody. Ah takes mine."

"Ah bet, Ah'll live to pick yo' bones, Brer Hawk."

"Aw, naw, you won't, Brer Buzzard. Watch me git my livin'."

He seen a sparrer sittin' on a dead limb of a tree and he sailed off and dived down at dat sparrer. De end of de limb was stickin' out and he run his breast right up on de sharp point and hung dere. De sparrer flew on off.

After while he got so weak he knowed he was gointer die. So de buzzard flew past just so — flyin' slow you know, and said, "Un hunh, Brer Hawk, Ah told you Ah was gointer live to pick yo' bones. Ah waits on de salvation of de Lawd."

●◆ Write a paragraph that summarizes what takes place in this folk tale. End by stating what you think is the lesson to be learned from the story.

Lesson to Be Learned:

Share your ideas about the lesson of the story with a partner. Try to apply the lesson to some current situations in the news or in your own lives, keeping in mind that fables reflect the lives and values of the people telling them.

●◆ Write a contemporary fable out of one of the current situations you discussed or another you think of. For example, your fable might illustrate two different attitudes about competition in sports, peer pressure, or a make-it-rich scheme. Choose two animals for the fable whose characteristics fit the role each will portray.

Three

Personification in Fables

In animal fables, the animals personify human emotions, speech, and traits. They talk, cry, cook, and marry. **Personification** is defined as the practice of giving human traits to things that are not human. For example, a heavy wind might be called a "slap in the face" or a gentle breeze referred to as a "caress." Read the following fable, noticing the particular human traits the animals personify.

No Tracks Coming Back
(African American Folk Tale)
collected by Arthur Huff Fauset

You know Brer Rabbit said to be the wisest animal in the forest. So Brer Rabbit was walkin' along one day when Brer Fox come along. "Say, Brer Rabbit," Brer Fox says, "ain't you goin' to de big meetin'? Everybody goin.' " "Zat so," says Brer Rabbit, "sure I'm goin.'" So Brer Fox went off an' Brer Rabbit he take an' look aroun'. Pretty soon he see hundreds o' footprints an' all goin' in de same direction. Den he see dey all rabbit tracks. "Mmm," says Brer Rabbit, "all dem tracks goin' dat way, an' not a single one comin' dis way. Dat ain't no place fo' me."

Response notes

List the human traits personified by Brer Rabbit and Brer Fox.

Brer Rabbit	Brer Fox

Try your hand at personification. Complete the clusters below. Pick a clever animal for cluster one and list its characteristics. Pick a strong, less cunning animal for cluster two and list its characteristics. Think about Brer Rabbit and Brer Fox as examples.

1.

2.

●◆ Write a fable in which an animal personifies traits of cunning that help him outwit a stronger opponent.

Flamingo
MOTEL

137

Four

The clever trickster who lives by his wits is one of the oldest mythological figures in the world. The trickster animal is often the underdog who personifies cunning and mischief. Through cleverness, tricksters escape, evade, or overcome many challenges. They also sink themselves into immense trouble with their tricks. Think of Road Runner's speed pitted against the coyote's attempts to set traps for him. Coyote always seems to end up with his fur fried while Road Runner spins off to another adventure. The audience is left laughing at the crumple. Other times, the trickster gives us a good laugh because of quick thinking and clever revenge. The following fable from the Ashanti tribe in West Africa shows two trickster characters in action.

"Anansi and His Visitor, Turtle" (West African Folk Tale)

←——Response notes——→

It was almost time for Sun to sink to his resting place when Turtle, tired and dusty from hours of wandering, came to Anansi's house in the middle of a clearing in the woods. Turtle was hungry and the appetizing aroma of freshly cooked fish and yams drew him to approach Anansi's door and to knock. Anansi jerked the door open. When he saw the tired stranger he was inwardly annoyed, but it was an unwritten law of his country that one must never, no never, refuse hospitality to a passer-by.

Anansi smiled grimly and said, "Come in, come in, and share my dinner, Mr. Turtle."

As Turtle stretched out one paw to help himself from the steaming platter Anansi almost choked on a mouthful of food. In a shocked voice he said, "Turtle, I must remind you that in my country it is ill-mannered to come to the table without first washing. Please go to the stream at the foot of the hill and wash your dusty paws."

Turtle waddled down the hill and waded in the water for a while. He even washed his face. By the time he had trudged back up the trail to Anansi's house, the platter of fish was half empty. Anansi was eating at a furious rate.

Turtle stretched out one paw to help himself to food but again Anansi stopped him. "Turtle, your paws are still dusty. Please, go wash them."

"It is the dust from the long trail up the hill," Turtle explained in a meek voice. Clearly, it was not Turtle's place to argue if he expected to share the delectable meal, so he crawled down the hill a second time and rewashed his paws. Turtle was careful to walk on the grass beside the dusty trail on the climb back to Anansi's house. He hurried, for by now he was ravenous.

But, oh dear! Anansi had scraped the platter bare of fish and yams. "My, that was a good dinner," he said, wiping the last drop of gravy from his chin.

"Thank you for your wonderful hospitality, Anansi. Some day you must visit me." And Turtle, in a huff, went on home.

Some months later Anansi visited Turtle. After creepy crawling all

138

"Anansi and His Visitor, Turtle" (West African Folk Tale)

day from one tall grass stem to the next he found Turtle snoozing beside the river.

"Well, well," exclaimed Turtle. "So you have come to share my dinner. Make yourself comfortable, my dear Anansi, while I go below and prepare the food." He plunged into the river with a splash. Anansi was hungry. He paced the shore line and watched for Turtle's reappearance.

At last Turtle's head popped above the water. "Dinner is ready," he called as he bit into a huge clam. "Come on down." Then he disappeared from sight.

Anansi dived head first into the water, sank a few inches, then floated to the surface. His spindly legs and tiny body prevented him from sinking. He flipped and flapped his puny arms, tried swallow dives and belly flops, but he could not reach the bed of the river.

Then that cunning spider schemed. He filled the pockets of his jacket with small round pebbles, dived into the river, and sank with a bump that landed him right at the dinner table. Before him was spread the most delicious meal he had ever seen. There were oysters and clams, mussels, slices of eel, and crabs. As a centerpiece, sprays of watercress rested against large pink shrimp. Anansi's eyes widened with pleasure, his stomach rumbled in anticipation.

Turtle, already seated at the table, swallowed a piece of eel, looked at Anansi and said, "Oh, Anansi, I must remind you that in my country it is ill-mannered to come to the table wearing a jacket. Please take it off."

Very slowly Anansi removed his jacket. Very slowly Anansi left the table. Without the weight of the pebbles to hold him down he floated straight up through the green water and out of sight.

When you set out to outsmart another person to your own advantage, there is usually someone who can outsmart you.

What happened to Anansi's cunning and foresight when he goes to Turtle's home? Turtle seems cleverer on his own turf than he did on Anansi's. Now that both have outsmarted the other, what can possibly happen next? List several possibilities for future episodes.

example: Anansi invites Turtle and his enemy Alligator to a party.

Choose one of your possible continuations and write another episode about Anansi and Turtle. Both have the wits to outsmart the other in certain situations. You will need to create a circumstance where they will meet again. Because we know that each seems clever in his own environment, have the episode take place on new territory for both of them.

140

The trickster is a unique character in stories, personifying many of the darker aspects of human nature, but doing so with humor and wit.

Five Stories of Animals Today

In animal fables we learn about human nature from animals who talk and act and think and succeed and fail in the same ways that we do. Naturalists often equate animal behavior to human actions. Terry Tempest Williams does this in her book *Refuge*, a chronicle of the ecological effects of the rising water of the Great Salt Lake.

"Peregrine Falcon" from ***Refuge*** by Terry Tempest Williams

Lake Level: 4205.40'

← *Response notes* →

Not far from the Great Salt Lake is the municipal dump. Acres of trash heaped high. Depending on your frame of mind, it is either an olfactory fright show or a sociological gold mine. Either way, it is best to visit in winter.

For the past few years, when the Christmas Bird Count comes around, I seem to be relegated to the landfill. The local Audubon hierarchy tell me I am sent there because I know gulls. The truth lies deeper. It's an under-the-table favor. I am sent to the dump because secretly they know I like it.

As far as birding goes, there's often no place better. Our urban wastelands are becoming wildlife's last stand. The great frontier. We've moved them out of town like all other "low-income tenants."

The dump where I count birds for Christmas used to have cattails—but I can't remember them. A few have popped up below the hill again, in spite of bulldozers, providing critical covers for coots, mallards, and a variety of other waterfowl. I've seen herons standing by and once a snowy egret, but for the most part, the habitat now is garbage, perfect for starlings and gulls.

I like to sit on the piles of unbroken Hefties, black bubbles of sanitation. It provides comfort with a view. Thousands of starlings cover refuse with their feet. Everywhere I look—feathered trash. The starlings gorge themselves, bumping into each other like drunks. They are not discretionary. They'll eat anything, just like us. Three starlings picked a turkey carcass clean. Afterward, they crawled inside and wore it as a helmet. A carcass with six legs walking around—you have to be sharp counting birds at the dump.

I admire starlings' remarkable adaptability. Home is everywhere. I've seen them nesting under awnings on New York's Fifth Avenue, as well as inside aspen trunks in the Teton wilderness. Over 50 percent of their diet is insects. They are the most effective predators against the clover weevil in America.

Starlings are also quite beautiful if looked at with beginner's eyes. In autumn and winter, their plumage appears speckled, unkempt. But by spring, the lighter tips of their feathers have been worn away, leaving them with a black, glossy plumage, glistening with iridescences.

Inevitably, students at the museum will describe an elegant, black bird with flashes of green, pink, and purple.

"About this big," they say (holding their hands about seven inches apart vertically). "With a bright yellow bill. What is it?"

"A starling," I answer.

What follows is a dejected look flushed with embarrassment.

"Is that all?"

The name precedes the bird.

I understand it. When I'm out at the dump with starlings, I don't want to like them. They are common. They are aggressive, and they behave poorly, crowding out other birds. When a harrier happens to cross over from the marsh, they swarm him. He disappears. They want their trash to themselves.

Perhaps we project on to starlings that which we deplore in ourselves: our numbers, our aggressions, our greed, and our cruelty. Like starlings, we are taking over the world.

The parallels continue. Starlings forage by day in open country competing with native species such as bluebirds for food. They drive them out. In late afternoon they return in small groups to nest elsewhere, competing with cavity nesters such as clickers, martins, tree swallows, and chickadees. Once again, they move in on other birds' territories.

Starlings are sophisticated mimics singing songs of bobwhites, killdeer, flickers, and phoebes. Their flocks drape bare branches in spring with choruses of chatters, creeks, and coos. Like any good impostor, they confuse the boundaries. They lie.

What is the impact of such a species on the land? Quite simply, a loss of diversity.

What makes our relationship to starlings even more curious is that we loathe them, calling in exterminators because we fear disease, yet we do everything within our power to encourage them as we systematically erase the specialized habitats of specialized birds. I have yet to see a snowy egret spearing a bagel.

The man who wanted Shakespeare's birds flying in Central Park and altruistically brought starlings to America from England, is not to blame. We are—for creating more and more habitat for a bird we despise. Perhaps the only value in the multitudes of starlings we have garnished is that in some small way they allow us to comprehend what vast flocks of birds must have felt like.

The symmetry of starling flocks takes my breath away; I lose track of time and space. At the dump, all it takes is the sweep of my hand. They rise. Hundreds of starlings. They wheel and turn, twist and glide, with no apparent leader. They are the collective. A flight of frenzy. They are black stars against a blue sky. I watch them above the dump, expanding and contracting along the meridian of a winged universe.

Suddenly, the flock pulls together like a winced eye, then opens in an explosion of feathers. A peregrine falcon is expelled, but not without its prey. With folded wings he strikes a starling and plucks its body from mid-air. The flock blinks again and the starlings disperse,

"Peregrine Falcon" from **Refuge** by Terry Tempest Williams

one by one, returning to the landfill.

The starlings at the Salt Lake City municipal dump give us numbers that look good on our Christmas Bird Count, thousands, but they become faceless when compared to one peregrine falcon. A century ago, he would have seized a teal.

I will continue to count birds at the dump, hoping for under-the-table favors, but don't mistake my motives. I am not contemplating starlings. It is the falcon I wait for—the duckhawk with a memory for birds that once blotted out the sun.

←—Response notes—→

Look at the details that Williams uses to describe why the starlings flourish and the consequence of their numbers. List them below:

reasons why starlings flourish:

....

....

....

....

....

....

....

consequences:

....

....

....

....

....

....

....

....

....

143

●❖ Write about the lessons that you learned from Williams's observations about starlings and the peregrine falcon. How do they relate to human actions in the world?

Writers still link stories about the animal world with human behavior, even if these stories are not fables.

Transforming Stories

In an essay on the artistic impulse, former U.S. Poet Laureate Robert Haas wrote, "The first fact of the world is that it repeats itself. I had been taught to believe that the freshness of children lay in their capacity for wonder at the vividness and strangeness of the particular, but what is fresh in them is that they still experience the power of repetition." Haas is talking about the way we view the world around us and

how we respond to the familiar. Many writers use our expectations against us by retelling familiar events and stories with different endings or emphases.

Stories reflect the values, questions, and aspirations of a culture. The older, mythic stories retain their power because their messages reflect central concerns that are important regardless of time or place. Stories of journeys into the unknown, of temptations, tragedies,

human strengths or frailties are familiar to all people throughout history. Writers retell these stories in new ways because the themes and symbols are still important. The subject or themes a writer borrows from older stories take on new variations when transformed. The variations reflect and highlight our changing values and beliefs.

We learn to interpret meaning from the world around us, in part, because of the stories we have heard or read. Stories teach us how to look for significance in what takes place. But, a story can change as new information is added or as we try to understand the meaning of what has happened. As you read the following story by Gabriel García Márquez, think about the factors that influence why and how the villagers create a story out of a corpse that has washed up on their shore.

"The Handsomest Drowned Man in the World" by Gabriel García Márquez

←—Response notes—→

The first children who saw the dark and slinky bulge approaching through the sea let themselves think it was an enemy ship. Then they saw it had no flags or masts, and they thought it was a whale. But when it washed up on the beach, they removed the clumps of seaweed, the jellyfish tentacles, and the remains of fish and flotsam, and only then did they see that it was a drowned man.

They had been playing with him all afternoon, burying him in the sand and digging him up again, when someone chanced to see them and spread the alarm in the village. The men who carried him to the nearest house noticed that he weighed more than any dead man they had ever known, almost as much as a horse, and they said to each other that maybe he'd been floating too long and the water had got into his bones. When they laid him on the floor they said he'd been taller than all other men because there was barely enough room for him in the house, but they thought that maybe the ability to keep on growing after death was part of the nature of certain drowned men. He had the smell of the sea about him and only his shape gave one to suppose that it was the corpse of a human being, because the skin was covered with a crust of mud and scales.

They did not even have to clean off his face to know that the dead man was a stranger. The village was made up of only twenty-odd wooden houses that had stone courtyards with no flowers and which were spread about on the end of a desertlike cape. There was so little land that mothers always went about with the fear that the wind would carry off their children and the few dead that the years had caused among them had to be thrown off the cliffs. But the sea was calm and bountiful and all the men fit into seven boats. So when they found the drowned man they simply had to look at one another to see that they were all there.

That night they did not go out to work at sea. While the men went to find out if anyone was missing in neighboring villages, the women stayed behind to care for the drowned man. They took the mud off with grass swabs, they removed the underwater stones entangled in his hair, and they scraped the crust off with tools used for scaling fish. As they were doing that, they noticed that the vegetation on him came from faraway oceans and deep water and that his clothes were in tatters, as if he had sailed through labyrinths of coral. They noticed

146

← Response notes →

too that he bore his death with pride, for he did not have the lonely look of other drowned men who came out of the sea or that haggard, needy look of men who drowned in rivers. But only when they finished cleaning him off did they become aware of the kind of man he was and it left them breathless. Not only was he the tallest, strongest, most virile, and best built man they had ever seen, but even though they were looking at him there was no room for him in their imagination.

They could not find a bed in the village large enough to lay him on nor was there a table solid enough to use for his wake. The tallest men's holiday pants would not fit him, nor the fattest ones' Sunday shirts, nor the shoes of the one with the biggest feet. Fascinated by his huge size and his beauty, the women then decided to make him some pants from a large piece of sail and a shirt from some bridal brabant linen so that he could continue through his death with dignity. As they sewed, sitting in a circle and gazing at the corpse between stitches, it seemed to them that the wind had never been so steady nor the sea so restless as on that night and they supposed that the change had something to do with the dead man. They thought that if that magnificent man had lived in the village, his house would have had the widest doors, the highest ceiling, and the strongest floor, his bedstead would have been made from a midship frame held together by iron bolts, and his wife would have been the happiest woman. They thought that he would have had so much authority that he could have drawn fish out of the sea simply by calling their names and that he would have put so much work into his land that springs would have burst forth from among the rocks so that he would have been able to plant flowers on the cliffs. They secretly compared him to their own men, thinking that for all their lives theirs were incapable of doing what he could do in one night, and they ended up dismissing them deep in their hearts as the weakest, meanest, and most useless creatures on earth. They were wandering through that maze of fantasy when the oldest woman, who as the oldest had looked upon the drowned man with more compassion than passion, sighed:

"He has the face of someone called Esteban."

It was true. Most of them had only to take another look at him to see that he could not have any other name. The more stubborn among them, who were the youngest, still lived for a few hours with the illusion that when they put his clothes on and he lay among the flowers in patent leather shoes his name might be Lautaro. But it was a vain illusion. There had not been enough canvas, the poorly cut and worse sewn pants were too tight, and the hidden strength of his heart popped the buttons on his shirt. After midnight the whistling of the wind died down and the sea fell into its Wednesday drowsiness. The silence put an end to any last doubts: he was Esteban. The women who had dressed him, who had combed his hair, had cut his nails and shaved him were unable to hold back a shudder of pity when they had to resign themselves to his being dragged along the ground. It was then that they understood how unhappy he must have been with that

147

←—Response notes —→

huge body since it bothered him even after death. They could see him in life, condemned to going through doors sideways, cracking his head on crossbeams, remaining on his feet during visits, not knowing what to do with his soft, pink, sea lion hands while the lady of the house looked for her most resistant chair and begged him, frightened to death, sit here, Esteban, please, and he, leaning against the wall, smiling, don't bother, ma'am, I'm fine where I am, his heels raw and his back roasted from having done the same thing so many times whenever he paid a visit, don't bother, ma'am, I'm fine where I am, just to avoid the embarrassment of breaking up the chair, and never knowing perhaps that the ones who said don't go, Esteban, at least wait till the coffee's ready, were the ones who later on would whisper the big boob finally left, how nice, the handsome fool has gone. That was what the woman were thinking beside the body a little before dawn. Later, when they covered his face with a handkerchief so that the light would not bother him, he looked so forever dead, so defenseless, so much like their men that the first furrows of tears opened in their hearts. It was one of the younger ones who began the weeping. The others, coming to, went from sighs to wails, and the more they sobbed the more they felt like weeping, because the drowned man was becoming all the more Esteban for them, and so they wept so much, for he was the most destitute, most peaceful, and most obliging man on earth, poor Esteban. So when the men returned with the news that the drowned man was not from the neighboring villages either, the women felt an opening of jubilation in the midst of their tears.

"Praise the Lord," they sighed, "he's ours!"

The men thought the fuss was only womanish frivolity. Fatigued because of the difficult nighttime inquiries, all they wanted was to get rid of the bother of the newcomer once and for all before the sun grew strong on that arid, windless day. They improvised a litter with the remains of foremasts and gaffs, tying it together with rigging so that it would bear the weight of the body until they reached the cliffs. They wanted to tie the anchor from a cargo ship to him so that he would sink easily into the deepest waves, where fish are blind and divers die of nostalgia, and bad currents would not bring him back to shore, as had happened with other bodies. But the more they hurried, the more the women thought of ways to waste time. They walked about like startled hens, pecking with the sea charms on their breasts, some interfering on one side to put a scapular of the good wind on the drowned man, some on the other side to put a wrist compass on him, and after a great deal of *get away from there, woman, stay out of the way, look, you almost made me fall on top of the dead man*, the men began to feel mistrust in their livers and started grumbling about why so many main-altar decorations for a stranger, because no matter how many nails and holy-water jars he had on him, the sharks would chew him all the same, but the women kept piling on their junk relics, running back and forth, stumbling, while they released in sighs what they did not in tears, so that the men finally exploded with *since*

148

"The Handsomest Drowned Man in the World" by Gabriel García Márquez

← Response notes →

when has there ever been such a fuss over a drifting corpse, a drowned nobody, a piece of cold Wednesday meat. One of the women, mortified by so much lack of care, then removed the handkerchief from the dead man's face and the men were left breathless too.

He was Esteban. It was not necessary to repeat it for them to recognize him. If they had been told Sir Walter Raleigh, even they might have been impressed with his gringo accent, the macaw on his shoulder, his cannibal-killing blunderbuss, but there could be only one Esteban in the world and there he was, stretched out like a sperm whale, shoeless, wearing the pants of an undersized child, and with those stony nails that had to be cut with a knife. They only had to take the handkerchief off his face to see that he was ashamed, that it was not his fault that he was so big or so heavy or so handsome, and if he had known that this was going to happen, he would have looked for a more discreet place to drown in, seriously, I even would have tied the anchor off a galleon around my neck and staggered off a cliff like someone who doesn't like things in order not to be upsetting people now with this Wednesday dead body, as you people say, in order not to be bothering anyone with this filthy piece of cold meat that doesn't have anything to do with me. There was so much truth in his manner that even the most mistrustful men, the ones who felt the bitterness of endless nights at sea fearing that their women would tire of dreaming about them and begin to dream of drowned men, even they and others who were harder still shuddered in the marrow of their bones at Esteban's sincerity.

That was how they came to hold the most splendid funeral they could conceive of for an abandoned drowned man. Some women who had gone to get flowers in neighboring villages returned with other women who could not believe what they had been told, and those women went back for more flowers when they saw the dead man, and they brought more and more until there were so many flowers and so many people that it was hard to walk about. At the final moment it pained them to return him to the waters as an orphan and they chose a father and mother from among the best people, and aunts and uncles and cousins, so that through him all the inhabitants of the village became kinsmen. Some sailors who heard the weeping from a distance went off course and people heard of one who had himself tied to the mainmast, remembering ancient fables about sirens. While they fought for the privilege of carrying him on their shoulders along the steep escarpment by the cliffs, men and women became aware for the first time of the desolation of their streets, the dryness of their courtyards, the narrowness of their dreams as they faced the splendor and beauty of their drowned man. They let him go without an anchor so that he could come back if he wished and whenever he wished, and they all held their breath for the fraction of centuries the body took to fall into the abyss. They did not need to look at one another to realize that they were no longer all present, that they would never be. But they also knew that everything would be different from then on, that their houses would have wider doors, higher

149

© GREAT SOURCE. ALL RIGHTS RESERVED.

←—Response notes—→ ceilings, and stronger floors so that Esteban's memory could go everywhere without bumping into beams and so that no one in the future would dare whisper the big boob finally died, too bad, the handsome fool has finally died, because they were going to paint their house fronts gay colors to make Esteban's memory eternal and they were going to break their backs digging for springs among the stones and planting flowers on the cliffs so that in future years at dawn the passengers on great liners would awaken, suffocated by the smell of gardens on the high seas, and the captain would have to come down from the bridge in his dress uniform, with his astrolabe, his pole star, and his row of war medals and, pointing to the promontory of roses on the horizon, he would say in fourteen languages, look there, where the wind is so peaceful now that it's gone to sleep beneath the beds, over there, where the sun's so bright that the sunflowers don't know which way to turn, yes, over there, that's Esteban's village.

●◆ How does the event of a body washing up on shore expand and change into the story of Esteban? Write a few sentences that describe how the following factors contributed to the transformation of the corpse into Esteban.

1. Physical Characteristics of the Drowned Man

150

2. Location of the Village

3. The Women

4. Rituals for Burial

5. Village After Burial

> Stories evolve over time. They reflect the questions and challenges that various people face and how those are interpreted.

Recasting a Story

Writers often recast old stories into their own versions. Recasting means changing the form or content while keeping what is important in the original. It is one way for a writer to rethink the themes or ideas of a story.

●◆ Recast the events of García Márquez's story of Esteban into another version. Imagine that you have been hired to write a song for school children in the village of Esteban some 50 years after the incident. This song is intended to educate elementary schoolchildren into the legend of Esteban for whom their village has been named. The village council has asked you to create lyrics for a song about Esteban that conveys his legendary qualities.

Share your lyrics with a partner. Compare what you chose to emphasize in the legend.

Reinterpretations

Sometimes writers recast stories simply to update the **setting**, characters, and the moral. But often a writer also wants to comment on the story and emphasize different **points of view**. In reinterpreting a story, a writer wants to make us see a traditional story in a different way; to question the received wisdom of right and wrong, good and bad. An example is the following poem by the Russian poet Anna Akhmatova. It retells the biblical story about Lot and his wife.

Response notes

Lot's Wife
Anna Akhmatova

And the just man trailed God's messenger,
His huge, light shape devoured the black hill.
But uneasiness shadowed his wife and spoke to her:
"It's not too late, you can look back still

At the red towers of Sodom, the place that bore you,
The square in which you sang, the spinning-shed,
At the empty windows of that upper storey
Where children blessed your happy marriage-bed."

Her eyes that were still turning when a bolt
Of pain shot through them, were instantly blind;
Her body turned into transparent salt,
And her swift legs were rooted to the ground.

Who mourns one woman in a holocaust?
Surely her death has no significance?
Yet in my heart she never will be lost,
She who gave up her life to steal one glance.

Read the poem aloud. With a partner, discuss what you understand about the poem so far. Speculate on what caused the death of Lot's wife. Are there hints from Akhmatova that help you decide? Then, reread the last stanza of the poem again. What point do you think Akhmatova is making?

●✦ Write a brief summary of the poem. What is it about? What do you know about Lot's wife and her situation? What is Akhmatova's point in telling this story?

Now read the original version of the story Akhmatova presents in her poem. It tells of the destruction of the twin cities Sodom and Gomorrah. Two angels visit Sodom and forewarn Lot about God's decision to destroy the cities. Lot is counseled to flee with his family. Within the story of the destruction of the cities is the brief mention of the fate of Lot's wife during the family's escape.

Genesis, 19:12-26

←— Response notes —→

The two men said to Lot, "If you have anyone else here—sons, daughters, sons-in-law, or any other relatives living in the city—get them out of here, because we are going to destroy this place. The Lord has heard the terrible accusations against these people and has sent us to destroy Sodom."

Then Lot went to the men that his daughters were going to marry, and said, "Hurry up and get out of here; the Lord is going to destroy this place." But they thought he was joking.

At dawn the angels tried to make Lot hurry. "Quick!" they said. "Take your wife and your two daughters and get out, so that you will not lose your lives when the city is destroyed." Lot hesitated. The Lord, however, had pity on him; so the men took him, his wife, and his two daughters by the hand and led them out of the city. Then one of the angels said, "Run for your lives! Don't look back and don't stop in the valley. Run to the hills, so that you won't be killed."

But Lot answered, "No, please don't make us do that, sir. You have done me a great favor and saved my life. But the hills are too far away; the disaster will overtake me, and I will die before I get there. Do you see that little town? It is near enough. Let me go over there — you can see it is just a small place — and I will be safe."

He answered, "All right, I agree. I won't destroy that town. Hurry! Run! I can't do anything until you get there."

Because Lot called it small, the town was named Zoar.

The sun was rising when Lot reached Zoar. Suddenly the Lord rained burning sulfur on the cities of Sodom and Gomorrah and destroyed them and the whole valley, along with all the people there and everything that grew on the land. But Lot's wife looked back and was turned into a pillar of salt.

◆◆ Discuss with a partner what you see as the major differences between the biblical story and Akhmatova's poem. Then, write a paragraph describing the specific references that Akhmatova makes to the biblical passage and how her recasting is similar to and different from the original.

154

Four
Timeless Stories

Stories often take extra meaning from the periods in which they are written. For example, Wilfred Owen's famous poem "Dulce et Decorum Est" was written while he was fighting in World War I. It ironically refers to the old stories that glorified and celebrated war. Owen's circumstances caused him to see the old popular stories about war as destructive lies. Akhmatova, too, was suffering when she wrote her poem "Lot's Wife" sometime between 1922 and 1924. Russia was in the throes of a bloody revolution and writers like Akhmatova were hounded and attacked. What line in the poem seems to emphasize the turmoil and destruction that surrounded Akhmatova?

....

●◆ Write a paragraph explaining how your understanding of Akhmatova's poem changes when you know about her situation.

....
....
....

155

....
....

●◆ Keeping in mind the two versions, write about what this story means to you. What did you react to most? What issues in the situation were compelling and how did you feel the story connects with your life?

....
....
....
....
....
....
....

The same story will have different meanings and interpretations at different times in history.

y tales often inspire recastings by modern writers. The new stories depart from
the earlier versions to make us think anew about the ideas behind fairy tales. The
poet Randall Jarrell offers an example in his poem that reinterprets "Jack and the
Beanstalk."

●◆ Before reading the poem, write down what you remember about the story of
"Jack and the Beanstalk," including any details that come to mind. What do you
remember to be the moral of the story?

....

....

....

....

....

Sh...... ......membrances with others, and fill in as many details of the
...y as you can before you read "Jack" aloud with others.

Response notes

Jack
Randall Jarrell

The sky darkened watching you
And the year sinking in its journey
Seem to you the slit beanstalk
And the goose crumpled in its pen.

The river, the spilt boats,
And the giant like a cloud falling
Are all pieces in your mind
Of a puzzle that, once joined,

Might green again the rotting stack.
Now, the oven's stiff creaking
Vexes you, but lifelessly,
Shameless as someone else's dream;

The harp crying out as you ran
Seems, rustling, your daughter's yellow hair. . . .
As, bound in some terrible wooden charm,
You sit here rigid and aghast.

Sometimes, in your good memory,
The strait princess, the giant's simpler wife
Come torn and gazing, begging
The names you could never comprehend,

And in the narrowing circle, sitting
With the world's puzzle rusting in your hands,
You know then you can never regain
The land that the harp sang so loudly.

●◆ Reread the poem and then answer the following questions:

When in Jack's life does this version of the story occur?

What perspective is emphasized here that you don't remember from the fairy tale?

What do you think is Jarrell's point in this poem?

Stories can be retold from many perspectives. They may be told from the point of view of someone other than the original narrator. They may be told at a different point in the character's life. Write yet another version of Jack's story from another perspective. Then, explain your new interpretation of the original and how you connect to it.

Changes in perspective are another way of transforming older stories. These versions may change time period, speaker, setting, emphasis, or the moral of the story.

Asking Questions About Poems

Often people hesitate to ask questions because they think they will appear stupid. However, active readers know that questions are important. They help you understand what you read. Coming up with your own questions as you read is an excellent way to improve your understanding.

You may wonder: How can I ask questions if I don't understand a poem? What can I ask questions about? Are some questions better than others in helping me comprehend and interpret? You will find answers to those questions as you work on interpreting poems by asking questions. And you will find more questions, too.

Most poems, although quite different from each other, share common elements. If you want to understand the **literal** (word-for-word) meaning of a specific poem, you can begin with questions about some of the elements common to most poems. Read "A Blessing" by James Wright and consider the situation he describes.

Response notes

A Blessing
James Wright

Just off the highway to Rochester, Minnesota,
Twilight bounds softly forth on the grass.
And the eyes of those two Indian ponies
Darken with kindness.
They have come gladly out of the willows
To welcome my friend and me.
We step over the barbed wire into the pasture
Where they have been grazing all day, alone.
They ripple tensely, they can hardly contain their happiness
That we have come.
They bow shyly as wet swans. They love each other.
There is no loneliness like theirs.
At home once more,
They begin munching the young tufts of spring in the darkness.
I would like to hold the slenderer one in my arms.
For she has walked over to me
And nuzzled my left hand.
She is black and white,
Her mane falls wild on her forehead,
And the light breeze moves me to caress her long ear
That is delicate as the skin over a girl's wrist.
Suddenly I realize
That if I stepped out of my body I would break
Into blossom.

Write your initial impressions and questions in the response notes. Then, reread the poem to devise specific questions about three elements in the poem—the speaker, the situation, and the subject. A poem usually has a speaker, someone who expresses the ideas of the poem. The speaker may or may not be the poet, so it is important to look for whatever characteristics of the speaker the poet provides—age, interests, mood, appearance. Ask also about the situation—where the speaker is, whether he or she is with anyone, what time of day it is, what season of the year, who the speaker is talking to and why. Finally, consider the speaker's concerns, ideas, or goals—the subject of the poem.

160

●◆ In each box, write two or three questions that you could ask about this poem. Then, answer the questions with quotations from "A Blessing" or with your ideas about the poem.

Questions	Quotations/Knowledge
Speaker	
Situation	
What time of day is it?	"Twilight bounds softly off the grass"
Subject	

Asking questions about the speaker, the situation, and the subject of a poem will help you understand its literal meaning.

One aspect of active reading is looking at the ideas beyond the **literal** meaning. Think of a poem as being like an onion; each time you peel off a layer, there's another one beneath it. A more beautiful comparison might be the one that Naoshi Koriyama makes in "Unfolding Bud."

Response notes

Unfolding Bud
Naoshi Koriyama

One is amazed
By a water-lily bud
Unfolding
With each passing day,
Taking on a richer color
And new dimensions.

One is not amazed,
At a first glance,
By a poem,
Which is as tight-closed
As a tiny bud.

Yet one is surprised
To see the poem
Gradually unfolding,
Revealing its rich inner self,
As one reads it
Again
And over again.

➥ A good way to reveal the layers of meaning in a poem is to look at the comparisons the poet makes. In comparing a poem to a water-lily bud, Koriyama provides a different way to look at poems. Ask a question about this comparison that would help another reader to understand the poem. Then, write an answer for it. Avoid questions that would get a "yes or a no" response, such as "Does she compare a water-lily bud to a poem?" Instead, ask a question that could have more than one possible answer. For example, questions that begin "In what ways . . ." could have several answers.

question:

answer:

Now, go back to "A Blessing" by James Wright. Use the comparison technique to look for another layer of meaning in that poem. Reread the poem so that you can fill in the following chart. Note that Wright does not state all of his points of comparison; at least one of them is implied.

Object A	Object B	Questions about the comparison
The ponies bow	shyly as wet swans	How are the bows and the shyness like dating?
her long ear		
break into blossom		

What do you understand now about "The Blessing"? Review your questions to write a paragraph about the poem. Explain the literal meaning and then the second layer of meaning that you discovered.

Asking
questions
ut the
ons

Asking Interpretive Questions

I know that you need to ask questions that will help you understand the poem. But how can you tell helpful questions from unhelpful ones? Good interpretive questions should lead to answers that either reveal something that you did not know or confirm something you suspected but were not sure of.

One way to come up with effective questions is to think of interpreting a poem as having four steps. Ask questions for each of the steps:

1. *Collect* information—for example, speaker, situation, subject.

2. *Connect* the information you have into patterns or categories, seeing how the pieces of information are related.

3. *Construct* inferences or statements about the relationships you found among the bits of information.

4. Draw *conclusions* about the meanings of the poem. Poems may have more than one interpretation, so decide which conclusions are supported by the inferences and information.

Think about these steps as you read "A Man" by Nina Cassian.

Response notes

A Man
Nina Cassian

While fighting for his country, he lost an arm
and was suddenly afraid:
"From now on, I shall only be able to do things
    by halves.

I shall reap half a harvest.
I shall be able to play either the tune
or the accompaniment on the piano,
but never both parts together.
I shall be able to bang with only one fist
on doors, and worst of all
I shall only be able to half hold
my love close to me.
There will be things I cannot do at all,
applaud for example,
at shows where everyone applauds."

From that moment on, he set himself to do
everything with twice as much enthusiasm.
And where the arm had been torn away
a wing grew.

Generate one or two questions for each interpretive step. Write them in the boxes.

1. Questions to collect information

How is the speaker of the poem related to the man?

2. Questions to connect information

Why is it important that the man lost his arm while fighting for his country?

165

3. Questions to construct inferences

What can we tell about the man by knowing the things he fears he cannot do?

4. Questions to draw conclusions

What is Cassian suggesting about how to live?

●◆ Use the answers to your questions to write an interpretive paragraph. Begin with one of your conclusions about the meaning of the poem. Support it with your inferences and with details from the poem.

A series of
questions can

Four
Langu...

anguage and structure often provide additional information that you can use to make **inferences** about a poem's meanings. Some of the questions that you asked about previous poems probably involved language and structure, but you probably did not use those elements to help you interpret the meanings of the poems.

You will need to read "Every Good Boy Does Fine" by David Wagoner two or three times. Read it the first time to get a sense of the literal meaning of the poem.

Every Good Boy Does Fine
David Wagoner

I practiced my cornet in a cold garage
Where I could blast it till the oil in drums
Boomed back; tossed free throws till I couldn't move
    my thumbs;
Sprinted through tires, tackling a headless dummy.

In my first contest, playing a wobbly solo,
I blew up in the coda, alone on stage,
And twisting like my hand–tied necktie, saw the judge
Letting my silence dwindle down his scale.

At my first basketball game, gangling away from home
A hundred miles by bus to a dressing room,
Under the showering voice of the coach, I stood in a
    towel,
Having forgotten shoes, socks, uniform.

In my first football game, the first play under the
    lights
I intercepted a pass. For seventy yards, I ran
Through music and squeals, surging, lifting my cleats,
Only to be brought down by the safety man.

I took my second chances with less care, but in dreams
I saw the bald judge slumped in the front row,
The coach and team at the doorway, the safety man
Galloping loud at my heels. They watch me now.

You who have always horned your way through passages,
Sat safe on the bench while some came naked to court,
Slipped out of arms to win in the long run,
Consider this poem a failure, sprawling flat on a page.

167

Identify the situations of the poem by circling the events that the speaker participates in. Put a square around what he identifies as failures.

Reread the poem. This time collect information about the language. Identify the places where Wagoner uses words specific to each event, such as *coda*.

Now, use the information you have collected to ask and answer questions about the poem.

Structural Elements	Questions	Answers
title	What does the title remind me of?	This is the way I was taught to remember the names of the lines on the treble clef in music class.
number of stanzas (groups of lines separated by white space)		
the order of the things he sees in dreams when **168** he took his second chances		
Language Elements	Questions	Answers
words specific to a subject such as music or football		
words that signal a contrast such as "you"		

Studying language and structure will help you interpret a poem.

When you consider alternatives to elements of a poem, you can see better why the poet wrote as he or she did. Speculative questions can start in many ways. A common one is "What if . . . ?" They may start as statements, too, as in "I wonder why . . . ." With a partner, take a few minutes to brainstorm as many speculations as you can about one of the four poems you have read. For example, you might say "What if the animals in 'A Blessing' had been wolves?" Focus on such elements of the poem as speaker, situation, language, and so forth. Write your speculations in the response notes.

●◆ Now, select three of your speculations to explore further in one or two sentences each. To continue with the "wolves" example, you might write, "If the animals were wolves, they probably would not be as friendly and would not be happy that the speaker stopped."

1.

169

2.

3.

●◆ Now, select one of the speculations you just wrote. Write a new poem based on it. For example, if you were writing "A Blessing" about wolves, some of your lines might include, "The wolves sniff danger. Their nostrils flare, their fur bristles. We back away."

170

Text and Subtext

The old saying "there's more to this than meets the eye" is certainly true in reading. Active readers know that beneath every text is a subtext. The subtext is a collection of meanings implied by the author and supplied by the reader.

Readers must fill in the background of a story if it is not stated. They listen for the tone of voice that a speaker uses. They consider what is not said as much as what is. Critical readers do these things so naturally, they may not even realize that they are supplementing the meaning of the text.

Noticing the subtext may not come naturally at first, but you can learn to do it. You need to shift your focus from the words on the page to the meanings that surround them. Then you will realize that you are adding meaning to the author's words from your experiences and assumptions. Developing a conscious awareness of the subtext will make you a better reader.

Supplying the Background

One element of the subtext is the background of the characters and situation. An author may give you some background directly by saying, for example, "His parents were wealthy." Other aspects of the story's background may be implied. What kind of life do characters have outside the story? What has happened to them before we meet them? How have their experiences influenced their decisions? Active readers fill in this part of the subtext, attentive both to what is said and what is implied.

Read "Appointment with Love" the first time to understand the story and get an impression of the characters. You will need to read it a second time to begin supplying the background.

← Response notes →

"Appointment with Love" by S. I. Kishor

Six minutes to six, said the great round clock over the information booth in Grand Central Station. The tall young Army lieutenant who had just come from the direction of the tracks lifted his sunburned face, and his eyes narrowed to note the exact time. His heart was pounding with a beat that shocked him because he could not control it. In six minutes, he would see the woman who had filled such a special place in his life for the past thirteen months, the woman he had never seen, yet whose written words had been with him and sustained him unfailingly.

He placed himself as close as he could to the information booth, just beyond the ring of people besieging the clerks. . . .

Lieutenant Blandford remembered one night in particular, the worst of the fighting, when his plane had been caught in the midst of a pack of Zeros. He had seen the grinning face of one of the enemy pilots.

In one of his letters, he had confessed to her that he often felt fear, and only a few days before this battle, he had received her answer: "Of course you fear . . . all brave men do. Didn't King David know fear? That's why he wrote the Twenty-third Psalm. Next time you doubt yourself, I want you to hear my voice reciting to you: 'Yea, though I walk through the valley of the shadow of death, I shall fear no evil, for Thou art with me' . . ." And he had remembered; he had heard her imagined voice, and it had renewed his strength and skill.

Now he was going to hear her real voice. Four minutes to six. His face grew sharp.

Under the immense, starred roof, people were walking fast, like threads of color being woven into a gray web. A girl passed close to him, and Lieutenant Blandford started. She was wearing a red flower in her suit lapel, but it was a crimson sweet pea, not the little red rose they had agreed upon. Besides, this girl was too young, about eighteen, whereas Hollis Meynell had frankly told him she was thirty. "Well, what of it?" he had answered. "I'm thirty-two." He was twenty-nine.

His mind went back to that book—the book the Lord Himself must have put into his hands out of the hundreds of Army library books sent to the Florida training camp. *Of Human Bondage*, it was; and throughout the book were notes in a woman's writing. He had always

"Appointment with Love" by S. I. Kishor

hated that writing-in habit, but these remarks were different. He had never believed that a woman could see into a man's heart so tenderly, so understandingly. Her name was on the bookplate: Hollis Meynell. He had got hold of a New York City telephone book and found her address. He had written, she had answered. Next day he had been shipped out, but they had gone on writing.

For thirteen months, she had faithfully replied, and more than replied. When his letters did not arrive, she wrote anyway, and now he believed he loved her, and she loved him.

But she had refused all his pleas to send him her photograph. That seemed rather bad, of course. But she had explained: "If your feeling for me has any reality, any honest basis, what I look like won't matter. Suppose I'm beautiful. I'd always be haunted by the feeling that you had been taking a chance on just that, and that kind of love would disgust me. Suppose I'm plain (and you must admit that this is more likely) then I'd always fear that you were going on writing to me only because you were lonely and had no one else. No, don't ask for my picture. When you come to New York, you shall see me and then you shall make your decision. Remember, both of us are free to stop or to go on after that—whichever we choose. . . ."

One minute to six . . . he pulled hard on a cigarette.

Then Lieutenant Blandford's heart leaped higher than his plane had ever done.

A young woman was coming toward him. Her figure was long and slim; her blond hair lay back in curls from her delicate ears. Her eyes were blue as flowers, her lips and chin had a gentle firmness. In her pale green suit, she was like springtime come alive.

He started toward her, entirely forgetting to notice that she was wearing no rose, and as he moved, a small, provocative smile curved her lips.

"Going my way, soldier?" she murmured.

Uncontrollably, he made one step closer to her. Then he saw Hollis Meynell.

She was standing almost directly behind the girl, a woman well past forty, her graying hair tucked under a worn hat. She was more than plump; her thick-ankled feet were thrust into low-heeled shoes. But she wore a red rose in the rumpled lapel of her brown coat.

The girl in the green suit was walking quickly away.

Blandford felt as though he were being split in two, so keen was his desire to follow the girl, yet so deep was his longing for the woman whose spirit had truly companioned and upheld his own; and there she stood. Her pale, plump face was gentle and sensible; he could see that now. Her gray eyes had a warm, kindly twinkle.

Lieutenant Blandford did not hesitate. His fingers gripped the small, worn, blue leather copy of *Of Human Bondage* which was to identify him to her. This would not be love, but it would be something precious, something perhaps even rarer than love—a friendship for which he had been and must ever be grateful. . . .

He squared his broad shoulders, saluted and held the book out toward the woman, although even while he spoke he felt choked by

173

"Appointment with Love" by S. I. Kishor

←─ Response notes ─→

the bitterness of his disappointment.

"I'm Lieutenant John Blandford, and you—you are Miss Meynell. I'm so glad you could meet me. May—may I take you to dinner?"

The woman's face broadened in a tolerant smile. "I don't know what this is all about, son," she answered. "That young lady in the green suit—the one who just went by—begged me to wear this rose on my coat. And she said that if you asked me to go out with you, I should tell you that she's waiting for you in that big restaurant across the street. She said it was some kind of a test. I've got two boys with Uncle Sam myself, so I didn't mind to oblige you."

Are you surprised? Imagine how surprised Lieutenant Blandford must have been! Yet, both the text and the subtext prepare the reader for the ending. Reread the story and mark the places in the text where the author's description of the thoughts or actions of the characters suggests what will happen.

●◆ Write a diary entry from the **point of view** of Hollis Meynell. It should supply the events and attitudes in her background that might have made her suspicious of men liking her for her looks alone. The background could suggest why she set up the test for Lieutenant Blandford. Combine details from the story with details from your own experience and imagination to make this entry consistent with what you know about her.

174

> **Supplying the implied background for characters' actions is an important element of active reading.**

Two

Shifting Point of View

A writer carefully selects a narrator who will reveal what we know about the characters and events. In "Appointment with Love," the narrator tells only what Lieutenant Blandford thinks and feels. The reader must supply Hollis Meynell's thoughts based on the quotes from her letters. But, how would the story be different if the roles were reversed? What if the reader knew Hollis Meynell's thoughts but not Lieutenant Blandford's? Shifting the point of view is a good way for you to explore the subtext.

➜ Reread "Appointment with Love." Then, rewrite the story from Hollis Meynell's point of view. You may want to use the list of key events as an outline.

1. They start corresponding.
2. He confesses fear.
3. He asks for her picture.
4. They plan when and where to meet.
5. She sets up a test.
6. He passes it.

Read your story to a partner and discuss what your story adds to the situation Kishor described.

Three

Understanding Irony

I rony, or the contrast between expectation and reality, is also an element of the subtext. In some cases, you need to understand what is not being said in order to create a richer meaning. Verbal **irony**, the difference between what a writer or speaker says and what he or she means, plays a large role in "The Chaser" by John Collier. As you read the story, be alert to possible double meanings.

"The Chaser" by John Collier

← Response notes →

Alan Austen, as nervous as a kitten, went up certain dark and creaky stairs in the neighborhood of Pell Street, and peered about for a long time on the dim landing before he found the name he wanted written on one of the doors.

He pushed open this door, as he had been told to do, and found himself in a tiny room, which contained no furniture but a plain kitchen table, a rocking-chair, and an ordinary chair. On one of the dirty buff-coloured walls were a couple of shelves, containing in all perhaps a dozen bottles and jars.

An old man sat in the rocking-chair, reading a newspaper. Alan, without a word, handed him the card he had been given. "Sit down, Mr. Austen," said the old man very politely. "I am glad to make your acquaintance."

"Is it true," asked Alan, "that you have a certain mixture that has—er—quite extraordinary effects?"

"My dear sir," replied the old man, "my stock in trade is not very large—I don't deal in laxatives and teething mixtures—but such as it is, it is varied. I think nothing I sell has effects which could be precisely described as ordinary."

"Well, the fact is . . ." began Alan.

"Here, for example," interrupted the old man, reaching for a bottle from the shelf. "Here is a liquid as colourless as water, almost tasteless, quite imperceptible in coffee, wine, or any other beverage. It is also quite imperceptible to any known method of autopsy."

"Do you mean it is a poison?" cried Alan, very much horrified.

"Call it a glove-cleaner if you like," said the old man indifferently. "Maybe it will clean gloves. I have never tried. One might call it a lifecleaner. Lives need cleaning sometimes."

"I want nothing of that sort," said Alan.

"Probably it is just as well," said the old man. "Do you know the price of this? For one teaspoonful, which is sufficient, I ask five thousand dollars. Never less. Not a penny less."

"I hope all your mixtures are not as expensive," said Alan apprehensively.

"Oh dear, no," said the old man. "It would be no good charging that sort of price for a love potion, for example. Young people who need a love potion very seldom have five thousand dollars. Otherwise they would not need a love potion."

177

←—Response notes —→

"I am glad to hear that," said Alan.

"I look at it like this," said the old man. "Please a customer with one article, and he will come back when he needs another. Even if it is more costly. He will save up for it, if necessary."

"So," said Alan, "You really do sell love potions?"

"If I did not sell love potions," said the old man, reaching for another bottle, "I should not have mentioned the other matter to you. It is only when one is in a position to oblige that one can afford to be so confidential."

"And these potions," said Alan. "They are not just—just—er—"

"Oh, no," said the old man. "Their effects are permanent, and extend far beyond the mere casual impulse. But they include it. Oh, yes, they include it. Bountifully, insistently. Everlastingly."

"Dear me," said Alan, attempting a look of scientific detachment. "How very interesting!"

"But consider the spiritual side," said the old man.

"I do, indeed," said Alan.

"For indifference," said the old man, "they substitute devotion. For scorn, adoration. Give one tiny measure of this to the young lady—its flavour is imperceptible in orange juice, soup, or cocktails—and however gay and giddy she is, she will change altogether. She will want nothing but solitude and you."

"I can hardly believe it," said Alan. "She is so fond of parties."

"She will not like them any more," said the old man. "She will be afraid of the pretty girls you may meet."

"She will actually be jealous?" cried Alan in a rapture. "Of me?"

"Yes, she will want to be everything to you."

"She is, already. Only she doesn't care about it."

"She will, when she has taken this. She will care intensely. You will be her sole interest in life."

"Wonderful!" cried Alan.

"She will want to know all you do," said the old man. "All that has happened to you during the day. Every word of it. She will want to know what you are thinking about, why you smile suddenly, why you are looking sad."

"That is love!" cried Alan.

"Yes," said the old man. "How carefully she will look after you! She will never allow you to be tired, to sit in a draught, to neglect your food. If you are an hour late, she will be terrified. She will think you are killed, or that some siren has caught you."

"I can hardly imagine Diana like that!" cried Alan, overwhelmed with joy.

"You will not have to use your imagination," said the old man. "And, by the way, since there are always sirens, if by any chance you should, later on, slip a little, you need not worry. She will forgive you, in the end. She will be terribly hurt, of course, but she will forgive you—in the end."

"That will not happen," said Alan fervently.

"Of course not," said the old man. "But, if it did, you need not

178

worry. She would never divorce you. Oh, no! And, of course, she will
never give you the least, the very least, grounds for—uneasiness."

"And how much," said Alan, "is this wonderful mixture?"

"It is not as dear," said the old man, "as the glove-cleaner, or lifecleaner, as I sometimes call it. No. That is five thousand dollars, never
a penny less. One has to be older than you are, to indulge in that sort
of thing. One has to save up for it."

"But the love potion?" said Alan.

"Oh, that," said the old man, opening the drawer in the kitchen
table, and taking out a tiny, rather dirty-looking phial. "That is just a
dollar."

"I can't tell you how grateful I am," said Alan, watching him fill it.

"I like to oblige," said the old man. "Then customers come back,
later in life, when they are better off, and want more expensive
things. Here you are. You will find it very effective."

"Thank you again," said Alan. "Good-bye."

"Au revoir," said the old man.

A large part of the irony of this story is that the old man and the reader know
something that Alan does not. The thorough devotion he thinks he wants from Diana
will become suffocating. The old man does not echo Alan's "good-bye."
Instead, he says "au revoir," a French phrase that can mean "good-bye" but
also means "until we meet again." Find other examples of verbal irony to fill
in the chart.

What the old man says	What the old man suggests
au revoir	Alan will return for the glove cleaner

Understanding what is not said is essential to understanding a story, especially one that uses irony.

Four

In "The Chaser," Alan assumes that having Diana jealous of other women will be an advantage. The assumption that jealousy is a sign of true love is a common one. Yet, the old man does not appear to believe it. Often our assumptions guide our decisions, just as Alan's did. It can be helpful to shift **perspectives** and take a close look at the assumptions that are the basis for a story.

The authors of "Appointment with Love" and "The Chaser" made several assumptions about male-female relationships. For example, Lieutenant Blandford assumes that the man should be older than the woman, so he adds three years to his age when he writes Hollis Meynell. Your own assumptions are also a part of the subtext when you read. What do you assume about male-female relationships? Write down a few of your expectations regarding age, actions, and attitudes of males and females in romantic relationships.

Now, return to the two stories. In the response notes, try to identify the authors' assumptions about male-female relationships. Then, compare your assumptions to the ones the authors make. Write a paragraph in which you tell which story you like better. Is your preference influenced by the assumptions the author makes about male-female relationships? Do you prefer the story that is more similar or less similar to your own ideas?

What we understand and enjoy in our reading is often influenced by how much we share the author's assumptions about the subject.

Tone is the author's attitude toward the subject. To understand the **tone** of a work, you must be sensitive to a writer's choice of words. Read "One Perfect Rose" by Dorothy Parker.

Response notes

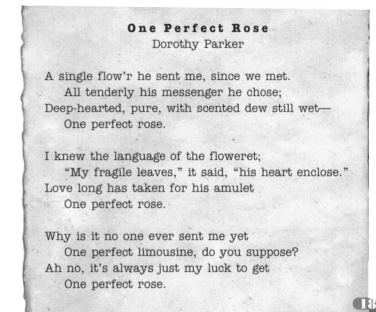

One Perfect Rose
Dorothy Parker

A single flow'r he sent me, since we met.
    All tenderly his messenger he chose;
Deep-hearted, pure, with scented dew still wet—
    One perfect rose.

I knew the language of the floweret;
    "My fragile leaves," it said, "his heart enclose."
Love long has taken for his amulet
    One perfect rose.

Why is it no one ever sent me yet
    One perfect limousine, do you suppose?
Ah no, it's always just my luck to get
    One perfect rose.

181

Parker used two kinds of words to achieve a contrast between old-fashioned romantic language and everyday speech. Notice how the meaning of "One perfect rose" changes from the first stanza to the last. What is the rose's value to the speaker? Discuss with a partner how you would read this poem aloud to show the speaker's change from a romantic tone to a cynical one. Then write two sentences describing Parker's tone and implications.

●✧ Now, rewrite the poem so that it has a different tone, such as solemn, formal, playful, and so on.

title:

Tone is an important aspect of the subtext. To understand it, pay attention to the author's words and what they imply.

Poetry and Craft

Poets choose forms the way most people choose clothes. It's partly style, partly personality, and partly occasion. Today, many poets write free verse, which has no rules. Other contemporary poets choose to write within the framework of traditional forms. Robert Frost once said that he would just as soon play tennis with the net down as he would write free verse. Here is a Frost poem on the subject of rhyme and meter:

In a Poem

The sentencing goes
    blithely on its way,
And takes the playfully
    objected rhyme
As surely as it keeps the
    stroke and time
In having its undeniable
    say.

Notice that Frost writes as if the "sentencing," the poem itself, is in control of the writing. Perhaps that is one of the appeals of form. Once writers start work on a ballad or a sonnet, they are committed to the form of the poem. As readers, we have expectations when we notice the shape of a poem. And while it's certainly possible to read a poem thoughtfully without consciously considering its form, it's not possible to read a poem without being affected by its form, whether we know it or not.

One Light Verse

> The trouble with a kitten is
> THAT
> Eventually it becomes a
> CAT.
> > Ogden Nash

Poems like those of Ogden Nash delight us and are easy to remember with their predictable **rhythm** and **rhyme**. Used in this way, rhyme and rhythm combine to form a type of **light verse**. It's nearly impossible to imitate Nash's **verse forms** without being light-hearted or funny. The **limerick** is a form of light verse that is fun to read and easy to imitate. Here are two limericks by unknown authors.

Response notes

Limericks

There was a young man of Bengal
Who went to a fancy dress ball.
He went just for fun
Dressed up as a bun,
And a dog ate him up in the hall.

There once was a man from Nantucket
Who kept all his cash in a bucket;
But his daughter named Nan
Ran away with a man,
And as for the bucket, Nantucket.

To analyze the verse form of a poem, you need to look at three things:

- rhyme scheme (the pattern of repeated sounds at the end of the **lines**)
- rhythm or **meter** (the number of **stresses** in each line)
- **stanza** pattern (the number of stanzas and the number of lines in each stanza)

RHYME SCHEME: To determine the rhyme scheme, underline the last word of each line. Use a small letter *a* to mark the sound of the first line. Every end word that has that sound will be an *a*. Use *b* for the next rhyming end word that has a different sound. The rhyme scheme for the limerick below is marked.

There was a young lady of Lynn   *a*
Who was so uncommonly thin   *a*
That when she essayed   *b*
To drink lemonade   *b*
She slipped through the straw and fell in.   *a*

Go back to the first two limericks. Underline and label the rhyming end words. Notice that the rhyme scheme for all three limericks is the same. This is the established pattern for this kind of light verse: aabba.

METER: the meter of a line is determined by the number of stressed syllables the line has. The names for metric lines of poetry are based on the Greek words for numbers. The most common metric lines are:

monometer: a line having one stress
dimeter: a line having two stresses
trimeter: a line having three stresses

tetrameter: a line having four stresses
pentameter: a line having five stresses
hexameter: a line having six stresses

Here is the sample limerick with the stresses marked to show how you sound it out or scan it.

There was | a young la | dy of Lynn	*three stresses or trimeter*
Who was | so uncom | monly thin	*three stresses or trimeter*
That when | she essayed	*two stresses or dimeter*
To drink | lemonade	*two stresses or dimeter*
She slipped | through the straw | and fell in.	*three stresses or trimeter*

Using the response notes, indicate how many stresses there are for each of the first two limericks. Read each line naturally and place marks on the **stressed syllables**. Count the number of stresses in each line and write the kind of meter beside the line.

You should find that all the limericks have the same meter. If you came up with a different pattern, go back and reread the lines. They should all fit the sample limerick pattern.

185

STANZA PATTERN: a stanza is a group of lines roughly making up a unit of thought. In a formal poem, the first stanza should set the pattern of rhyme and rhythm. Common stanza patterns are the **couplet** (two rhyming lines) and the **quatrain** (four lines, as in the Ogden Nash poem). Other forms, such as the **sonnet**, have a more complex pattern.

In the case of the limerick, there is just one stanza. If the three limericks had been part of a sequence, each dealing with the same subject, then each limerick would be considered one stanza.

● Now write a limerick of your own. Beneath each line of the sample limerick below, write your own line. Be sure to keep the rhythm of the original pattern.

There was a young lady of Niger

....

Who smiled as she rode on a tiger;

....

They returned from the ride

....

With the lady inside,

....

And the smile on the face of the tiger.

....

Here is a poem written by William Meredith, a Pulitzer Prize-winning poet from New England.

Response notes

The Illiterate
William Meredith

Touching your goodness, I am like a man
Who turns a letter over in his hand
And you might think this was because the hand
Was unfamiliar but, truth is, the man
Has never had a letter from anyone;
And now he is both afraid of what it means
And ashamed because he has no other means
To find out what it says than to ask someone.

His uncle could have left the farm to him,
Or his parents died before he sent them word,
Or the dark girl changed and want him for beloved.
Afraid and letter-proud, he keeps it with him.
What would you call his feeling for the words
That keep him rich and orphaned and beloved?

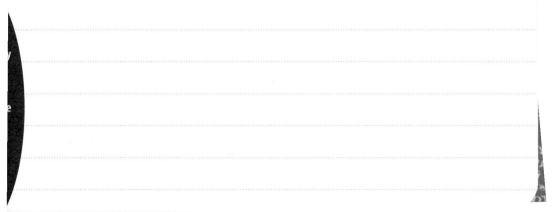

Notice the two uses of the word *hand*. The first means an actual hand; the second refers to a person's handwriting. ("He writes in a good hand" means that he has clear handwriting.)

Discuss these questions with a partner or small group:

- What are the possibilities that the letter carries?
- Do you think the poet is talking about a man who receives an actual letter or about the narrator himself?
- What is the narrator saying about himself in "Touching your goodness, I am like a man who. . .?"

Look again at the title of the poem. Write down ideas or questions about the title's meaning.

The Italian Sonnet

The poem you read in the previous lesson, "The Illiterate," is written in a poetic form that is very popular with contemporary as well as older poets— the **sonnet**. One of the things that makes this poem easy to read is that its meter is iambic **pentameter**, the meter of everyday spoken English. The basis of meter is the **foot**, a combination of two or three syllables. The **iamb** is the most common individual poetic foot; it has two syllables with the stress on the second one. An example of an iamb is the word *today*, which we pronounce with the stress on the second syllable. The opposite of an iamb is the **trochee**, which has the stressed syllable first, as in *sandwich* or *power*. Iambic pentameter, with a number of trochaic variations, is the meter of the sonnet as well as of a lot of other poetry. Shakespeare, for example, wrote most of his plays in unrhymed iambic pentameter, which is known as **blank verse**. The sonnet, however, uses specific **rhyme** and **stanza** patterns.

Here is the rhyme scheme for "The Illiterate." It is not necessary, in the rules for the sonnet, to repeat actual words as Meredith does. The rhyme scheme looks the same regardless.

The Illiterate
William Meredith

Response notes

Touching your goodness, I am like a man   *a*
Who turns a letter over in his hand   *b*
And you might think this was because the hand   *b*
Was unfamiliar but, truth is, the man   *a*
Has never had a letter from anyone;   *c*
And now he is both afraid of what it means   *d*
And ashamed because he has no other means   *d*
To find out what it says than to ask someone.   *c*

His uncle could have left the farm to him,   *e*
Or his parents died before he sent them word,   *f*
Or the dark girl changed and want him for beloved.   *g*
Afraid and letter-proud, he keeps it with him.   *e*
What would you call his feeling for the words   *f*
That keep him rich and orphaned and beloved?   *g*

"The Illiterate" is an example of a kind of sonnet known as a "Petrarchan," or Italian sonnet. There is some flexibility in the rhyme scheme. Traditionally, its rhyme scheme is abbaabba cdecde. Meredith has used a variation, but he has been true to the distinction of the two stanzas. In the traditional Italian sonnet, the first stanza sets forth a situation and the second comments on it.

➥ What is the situation set forth in the first eight lines?

....

....

....

....

➥ What does the narrator say about the situation in the last six lines?

....

....

....

....

➥ Look at the form of this poem and analyze how the form is related to the meaning. What does this add to your understanding of the title of the poem?

....

....

....

....

....

....

....

....

....

The sonnet is a fourteen-line poem which establishes a situation and then comments on it.

Four

The Shakespearean Sonnet

The Shakespearean **sonnet**, like the Italian, is a fourteen-line poem **written in iambic pentameter**. It differs, however, in its organization of thought: three **quatrains** develop a **central idea** or **argument**, and a **couplet** provides some kind of conclusion. The **rhyme** scheme creates the pattern, as you can see from one of Shakespeare's most famous sonnets.

Sonnet 116
William Shakespeare

Let me not to the marriage of true minds — *a*
Admit impediments. Love is not love — *b*
Which alters when it alteration finds, — *a*
Or bends with the remover to remove: — *b*
Oh, no! it is an ever-fixed mark, — *c*
That looks on tempests and is never shaken; — *d*
It is the star to every wandering bark, — *c*
Whose worth's unknown, although his height be taken. — *d*
Love's not Time's fool, though rose lips and cheeks — *e*
Within his bending sickle's compass come; — *f*
Love alters not with his brief hours and weeks, — *e*
But bears it out even to the edge of doom. — *f*
If this be error and upon me proved, — *g*
I never writ, nor no man ever loved. — *g*

Response notes

Imagine that this is an essay with a thesis statement, an argument, and a conclusion. Analyze the way the thought pattern progresses through the three quatrains and the couplet.

First quatrain: What point does the speaker make about love?

Second quatrain: To what does the speaker compare love? How does the comparison show what the speaker thinks about love?

Third quatrain: How does the speaker use the negative to say what love is?

Couplet: How do the final two lines provide a feeling of conclusion to the argument?

In a more contemporary Shakespearean sonnet, Edna St.
the same subject: love.

Response notes

Pity Me Not
Edna St. Vincent Millay

Pity me not because the light of day
At close of day no longer walks the sky;
Pity me not for beauties passed away
From field and thicket as the year goes by;
Pity me not the waning of the moon,
Nor that the ebbing tide goes out to sea,
Nor that a man's desire is hushed so soon,
And you no longer look with love on me.
This have I known always: Love is no more
Than the wide blossom which the wind assails,
Than the great tide that treads the shifting shore,
Strewing fresh wreckage gathered in the gales:
Pity me that the heart is slow to learn
What the swift mind beholds at every turn.

190

Using the guidelines from your analysis of Shakespeare's sonnet, analyze Millay's poem. Focus on two points:

• the way the pattern of the poem underscores the points of her argument
• the way the two poems develop the ideas of what love is

The organization of the Shakespearean sonnet provides a basis for posing a question or idea and then providing a resolution in the final two lines.

GREAT SOURCE. ALL RIGHTS RESERVED.

Five The Modern Sonnet

Poets today take a lot of liberties with the traditional forms of the **sonnet**. Some make poems of thirteen lines, some shorten the lines to **tetrameter** (four feet) instead of **pentameter** (five feet). Many have given up the **rhyme** scheme entirely. Still, they maintain the basic structure that provides an organization to their ideas. Read "I Really Do Live by the Sea" by Barbara Greenberg.

I Really Do Live by the Sea
Barbara Greenberg

Response notes

I really do live by the sea. I really am happy!
I really do have a vital, a permanent marriage
only death can undo. I do, I am. I really love
him. I really love you too, and a few close others.
My dear children, of course. And babies categorically.
And the natural world—believe me, I answer its beauty
the way the sea, in its colors, answers a complex sky.
One can feel into nature without being escapist, you know.
If ever I was an "as if" person, I'm not so now.
I seldom drift off. I'm here, alert, present.
I keep voting "aye" to my life, haven't you heard me?
That one family weekend when you saw me fall
into the abyss—that was a fluke, forget you saw that.
I really do live by the sea. I really am happy.

Look at Greenberg's use of the word *really*. What does the repetitious use of that word do to your interpretation of the meaning of the poem? Discuss this question with a classmate or group.

Compare the form of Greenberg's sonnet to that of the traditional sonnet.

Characteristics	Traditional sonnet	Greenberg's sonnet
Number of lines		
Line length		
Rhyme scheme		

© GREAT SOURCE. ALL RIGHTS RESERVED.

●◆ Reread the poems in this unit and explore the idea that **form**—structure, **rhythm**, and rhyme—allows a kind of freedom that the complete absence of rules does not. You may agree or disagree with this idea, but your argument must be based on examples. Use examples from the poems in this unit as well as your own responses to the rules that operate in your life.

Exploring your own ideas about form in poetry will help you become a more observant reader of poetry. It will also give you ideas about how to shape poems you might like to write yourself.

Writing from Models: Tone

When you analyze a writer's work, you need to be able to define tone. You need to be able to recognize what tone a writer creates and to account for how it is done.

One way to understand tone is through modeling. "Our habits make our style," said poet Josephine Miles. Modeling allows you to know something about the habits of writers. You begin to know something,

too, about your own habits, your own style. Modeling allows you to try out different authors' ways of creating specific effects. It allows you to see how structure and style are directly tied up with an author's ideas.

There are many ways of modeling. You can model a passage word for word; that is called an emulation. You can write a paralog, which is a dialogue with an author. You

can model a passage by imitating its tone or structure. By modeling, you won't just imitate others' styles; you will begin to explore what different styles are like. You will learn which ones come closest to how you like to express yourself. Style in writing, as in dress, evolves as we develop our personalities.

One Reading for Tone

Tone is the attitude or **point of view** a writer takes toward a subject and an audience. It is the emotional aspect of the work, which in speech is conveyed by **inflections** of the speaker's voice. In writing, we have no inflections, no body language to help us. We depend, instead, on **diction** (the kind of language the writer uses), on the connotations of words, and on elements such as **imagery**, **rhythm**, and **syntax**.

There is a large range of **tones** literature can have: dramatic, comic, formal, informal, serious, angry, playful, sad, joyful, affectionate, solemn, mocking, reverent, calm, or excited. There are always others, as human emotion is a broad category.

When we speak of a person's "tone of voice," we are close to understanding what is meant by tone in a poem. Read "The Unknown Citizen" by W. H. Auden. Make notations about the tone of the poem. You will hear the tone better if you read it aloud or listen to someone else reading it.

Response notes

94

The Unknown Citizen
W. H. Auden
*(To JS/07/M/378
This Marble Monument
Is Erected by the State)*

He was found by the Bureau of Statistics to be
One against whom there was no official complaint,
And all the reports on his conduct agree
That, in the modern sense of an old-fashioned word, he
    was a saint,
For in everything he did he served the Greater
    Community.
Except for the War till the day he retired
He worked in a factory and never got fired,
But satisfied his employers, Fudge Motors Inc.
Yet he wasn't a scab or odd in his views,
For his Union reports that he paid his dues,
(Our report on his Union shows it was sound)
And our Social Psychology workers found
That he was popular with his mates and liked a drink.
The Press are convinced that he bought a paper every day
And that his reactions to advertisements were normal
    in every way.
Policies taken out in his name prove that he was fully
    insured.
And his health-card shows he was once in hospital but
    left it cured.
Both Producers Research and High-Grade Living declare
He was fully sensible to the advantages of the
    Installment Plan

And had everything necessary to the Modern Man,
A phonograph, a radio, a car and a frigidaire.
Our researchers into Public Opinion are content
That he held the proper opinions for the time of year;
When there was peace, he was for peace; when there
    was war, he went.
He was married and added five children to the
    population,
Which our Eugenist says was the right number for a
    parent of his generation.
And our teachers report that he never interfered with
    their education.
Was he free? Was he happy? The question is absurd:
Had anything been wrong, we should certainly have heard.

Response notes

●◆ Explain the tone and meaning of line 27: "And our teachers report that he
never interfered with their education."

●◆ What do you think is Auden's attitude in this poem?

●◆ Line 5 states that "in everything he did he served the Greater Community."
Auden follows this with a list of examples of how he served the Greater
Community. What are two additional ways that the "unknown citizen" might
have served the Greater Community? Write them to be inserted into the poem
between lines 27 and 28. Try to maintain the same tone that Auden establishes.

Good
readers are
alert to the
tone of voice
in a poem.
They read
between the
lines for
meaning.

Read the poem "You Understand the Requirements" by Lyn Lifshin. Annotate it with questions and ideas about the **tone**.

Response notes

You Understand the Requirements
Lyn Lifshin

We are
sorry to have to
regret to
tell you
sorry sorry
regret sorry that you have
failed

your hair should have been
piled up higher

you have failed to
pass failed
your sorry
regret your
final hair comprehensive
exam satisfactorily
you understand the requirements

you understand we are
sorry final
and didn't look as professional
as desirable
or sorry dignified
and have little enough
sympathy for 16th century
sorry english anglicanism
we don't know doctoral
competency what to think and
regret you will sorry not
be able to stay
or finish

final regret your disappointment
the unsuccessfully completed best
wishes for the future
it has been a
regret sorry the requirements
the university policy
please don't call us.

RULES of BEHAVIOR

Imagine that you have been interviewed for entrance into a university program. Your heart is set on this particular course of study. Now imagine that you have received a letter rejecting your application. You recognize right away ("We are sorry...) that you didn't get in. The rest of the letter is a blur. The words and sentences run together. All you can focus on is the rejection. Reread the poem with this scenario in mind.

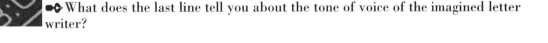Lines 14-21 contain words that would not be logical in a formal letter from a university ("hair," "didn't look as professional," "dignified"). What do these lines tell you about why the recipient thought she was rejected?

....

....

What does the last line tell you about the tone of voice of the imagined letter writer?

....

....

Imagine that you have been rejected for a job or place on a team that you really wanted. Write a short rejection letter as it might really look.

....

....

....

....

....

....

....

....

....

....

Consider how this rejection might read if you were upset. Use Lifshin's strategy of running ideas together and including things that are only in the mind of the recipient to create a reading of your letter.

Comparing Poems

Use the chart below to show the ways the poems by W. H. Auden and Lyn Lifshin are alike and different. In your analysis, consider similarities and differences in tone as achieved through the dramatic situation, **persona** (the person saying the lines), and sentence patterns or word choices.

Elements to be compared	Auden's poem	Similarities between the poems	Lyn Lifshin's poem
Tone			
Scenario			
Persona			
Sentence patterns and word choices			

●◆ Now look at the way the sentence patterns and word choice help convey **tone** in the poems. Be specific about the ways the writers helped you understand how the poems should be read.

Writ___ ___t up the tone ___ ___lishing a scena___ ___ Sent___ a___ ___ned

Four

Using Metaphors

In his book *Einstein's Dreams*, Alan Lightman imagines Albert Einstein as a young man dreaming about all the possibilities of time. Between chapters in which Einstein converses with a friend about his work, Lightman imagines Einstein's dreams. Each chapter describes a different quality of time. The following excerpt is from a chapter about time standing still. Annotate the reading as fully as you can. Particularly note the questions you have.

Response notes

from *Einstein's Dreams*
Alan Lightman

14 May 1905

There is a place where time stands still. Raindrops hang motionless in air. Pendulums of clocks float mid-swing. Dogs raise their muzzles in silent howls. Pedestrians are frozen on the dusty streets, their legs cocked as if held by strings. The aromas of dates, mangoes, coriander, cumin are suspended in space.

As a traveler approaches this place from any direction, he moves more and more slowly. His heartbeats grow farther apart, his breathing slackens, his temperature drops, his thoughts diminish, until he reaches dead center and stops. For this is the center of time. From this place, time travels outward in concentric circles—at rest at the center, slowly picking up speed at greater diameters.

Who would make pilgrimage to the center of time? Parents with children, and lovers.

And so, at the place where time stands still, one sees parents clutching their children, in a frozen embrace that will never let go. The beautiful young daughter with blue eyes and blond hair will never stop smiling the smile she smiles now, will never lose this soft pink glow on her cheeks, will never grow wrinkled or tired, will never get injured, will never unlearn what her parents have taught her, will never think thoughts that her parents don't know, will never know evil, will never tell her parents that she does not love them, will never leave her room with the view of the ocean, will never stop touching her parents as she does now.

And at the place where time stands still, one sees lovers kissing in the shadows of buildings, in a frozen embrace that will never let go. The loved one will never take his arms from where they are now, will never give back the bracelet of memories, will never journey far from his lover, will never place

Response notes

FROM ***EINSTEIN'S DREAMS*** (continued)

himself in danger in self-sacrifice, will never
fail to show his love, will never become jealous,
will never fall in love with someone else, will
never lose the passion of this instant in time.

No one can really experience time standing still. Lightman is trying to explain
ideas that can only be expressed through story or **metaphor**. He is describing a
series of events that would or would not happen in a timeless world. Timelessness is
described in terms of something else. Lightman uses the framework of a dream to
try to describe timelessness.

Lightman presents both positive and negative images. Mark the place in the text
where he shifts from positive to negative images.

➥ What images do you think most clearly convey the idea of timelessness? Jot down
two positive and two negative passages and tell why you chose them.

Passages that convey timelessness	Why I chose these lines

200

Writers
often use
metaphors to
explain complex
ideas or concepts
that are difficult
to explain.

© GREAT SOURCE. ALL RIGHTS RESERVED.

Five
The Paralog

In a paralog, you enter into a dialogue with the author. The prefix *para* means "by the side of" and the word root *log* or *logue* means "written or spoken language." So a paralog refers to a piece of writing in which a reader responds directly to the author, either line by line or section by section. The result is a piece of writing in two voices: the original author's and the respondent's. The one aspect that remains constant is the tone.

To begin your paralog, reread the excerpt from *Einstein's Dreams* in lesson four. Underline two or three phrases or sentences that you like, either for their meaning or for the mood they create. In the response notes section, write a phrase or sentence in response to each line you have underlined. Try to make your lines sound as if you are answering the phrases or sentences you have underlined. Two samples are written below for you.

from ***Einstein's Dreams***
Alan Lightman

<u>There is a place where time stands still</u>

<u>And so, at the place where time stands still, one sees parents clutching their children, in a frozen embrace that will never let go.</u>

Response notes

There is a place where it never stops raining. All the houses have steeply slanting roofs.

And so, here, in this land of the rainforest, parrots swing wildly on great swags of green moss.

201

Read what you have created as a whole. First read the underlined words, then your own. Read them phrase by phrase or sentence by sentence, as you would a dialogue. You can reconsider your choices from *Einstein's Dreams* and change any of your phrases or sentences to make the paralog read more smoothly. It is the consistency in tone that will make the paralog work.

When you're satisfied with the way it sounds, write it out as a paralog on the next page using the following pattern. Give your paralog a title.

Title
Words from *Einstein's Dreams*
Your words
Words from *Einstein's Dreams*
Your words
Words from *Einstein's Dreams*
    and so on. . .

title:

Writing a paralog lets you enter into a dialogue with an author. In this way you can expand your understanding of how writers create tone and mood.

Focus on the Writer: Zora Neale Hurston

A story about Zora Neale Hurston tells how she arrived at a reception in 1925 to receive a prize for her first published work, a play entitled *Color Struck*. Hurston, fashionably late, paused at the door, gave her scarf a toss around her throat, and boomed out, "Color-r-r Str-r-ruck!" She was dramatic, irreverent, and controversial, but never dull.

Hurston worked as an anthropologist and collected an extensive record of African American folklore, which was published in two volumes, *Mules and Men* and *Tell My Horse*. Alice Walker wrote that Hurston revealed "descendants of an inventive, joyous, courageous, and outrageous people; loving drama, appreciating wit, and, most of all, relishing the pleasure of each other's loquacious and bodacious company."

In her novels, short stories, essays, and plays, you will encounter life and experiences that range from the kitchen to the barnyard as Hurston draws images from the rural landscape of Florida where she was raised. Hurston's stories portray people who struggle to define themselves and their relationships with others within the larger world.

One

The Autobiographical Narrator

Some writers engage in sustained explorations of how their lives are connected to their writing. They become characters in their own work, taking on an **autobiographical** voice that is often as powerful as any of the characters they create in their fictional writing. Through **memoir**, Hurston tells us much about who she is and shares her aspirations and hopes. In an essay, Alice Walker wrote that Hurston "became an orphan at nine, a runaway at fourteen, a maid and manicurist (because of necessity and not from love of the work) before she was twenty, and—with one dress—managed to become Zora Neale Hurston, author and anthropologist."

In "How It Feels To Be Colored Me," written in 1928, Hurston reveals some of her personality traits and her understanding of how race influenced her evolving sense of self.

from **"How It Feels To Be Colored Me"** by Zora Neale Hurston

←— Response notes —→

I am colored but I offer nothing in the way of extenuating circumstances except the fact that I am the only Negro in the United States whose grandfather on the mother's side was *not* an Indian chief.

I remember the very day that I became colored. Up to my thirteenth year I lived in the little Negro town of Eatonville, Florida. It is exclusively a colored town. The only white people I knew passed through the town going to or coming from Orlando. The native whites rode dusty horses, the Northern tourists chugged down the sandy village road in automobiles. The town knew the Southerners and never stopped cane chewing when they passed. But the Northerners were something else again. They were peered at cautiously from behind curtains by the timid. The more venturesome would come out on the porch to watch them go past and got just as much pleasure out of the tourists as the tourists got out of the village.

The front porch might seem a daring place for the rest of the town, but it was a gallery seat to me. My favorite place was atop the gate-post. Proscenium box for a born first-nighter. Not only did I enjoy the show, but I didn't mind the actors knowing that I liked it. I actually spoke to them in passing. I'd wave at them and when they returned my salute, I would say something like this: "Howdy-do-well-I-thank-you-where-you-goin'?" Usually automobile or the horse paused at this, and after a queer exchange of compliments, I would probably "go a piece of the way" with them as we say in farthest Florida. If one of my family happened to come to the front in time to see me, of course negotiations would be rudely broken off. But even so, it is clear that I was the first "welcome-to-our-state" Floridian, and I hope the Miami Chamber of Commerce will please take notice.

During this period, white people differed from colored to me only in that they rode through town and never lived there. They liked to hear me "speak pieces" and sing and wanted to see me dance the parse-me-la, and gave me generously of their small silver for doing

from **"How It Feels To Be Colored Me"** by Zora Neale Hurston

←—Response notes—→

these things, which seemed strange to me for I wanted to do them so much that I needed bribing to stop. Only they didn't know it. The colored people gave no dimes. They deplored any joyful tendencies in me, but I was their Zora nevertheless. I belonged to them, to the nearby hotels, to the country—everybody's Zora.

But changes came in the family when I was thirteen, and I was sent to school in Jacksonville. I left Eatonville, the town of the oleanders, as Zora. When I disembarked from the riverboat at Jacksonville, she was no more. It seemed that I had suffered a sea change. I was not Zora of Orange County any more, I was now a little colored girl. I found it out in certain ways. In my heart as well as in the mirror, I became a fast brown—warranted not to rub nor run.

But I am not tragically colored. There is no great sorrow dammed up in my soul, nor lurking behind my eyes. I do not mind at all. I do not belong to the sobbing school of Negrohood who hold that nature somehow has given them a lowdown dirty deal and whose feelings are all hurt about it. Even in the helter-skelter skirmish that is my life, I have seen that the world is to the strong regardless of a little pigmentation more or less. No, I do not weep at the world—I am too busy sharpening my oyster knife. . . .

At certain times I have no race, I am *me*. When I set my hat at a certain angle and saunter down Seventh Avenue, Harlem City, feeling as snooty as the lions in front of the Forty-Second Street Library, for instance. So far as my feelings are concerned, Peggy Hopkins Joyce on the Boule Mich with her gorgeous raiment, stately carriage, knees knocking together in a most aristocratic manner, has nothing on me. The cosmic Zora emerges. I belong to no race nor time, I am the eternal feminine with its string of beads.

I have no separate feeling about being an American citizen and colored. I am merely a fragment of the Great Soul that surges within the boundaries. My country, right or wrong.

Sometimes, I feel discriminated against, but it does not make me angry. It merely astonishes me. How *can* any deny themselves the pleasure of my company! It's beyond me.

But in the main, I feel like a brown bag of miscellany propped against a wall. Against a wall in company with other bags, white, red and yellow. Pour out the contents, and there is discovered a jumble of small things priceless and worthless. A first-water diamond, an empty spool, bits of broken glass, lengths of string, a key to a door long since crumbled away, a rusty knife-blade, old shoes saved for a road that never was and never will be, a nail bent under the weight of things too heavy for any nail, a dried flower or two, still a little fragrant. In your hand is the brown bag. On the ground before you is the jumble it held—so much like the jumble in the bags, could they be emptied, that all might be dumped in a single heap and the bags refilled without altering the content of any greatly. A bit of colored glass more or less would not matter. Perhaps that is how the Great Stuffer of Bags filled them in the first place—who knows?

In what ways does Hurston define herself? As a way of starting to answer this question, list words or phrases that reveal how she sees herself at different points in her life:

Eatonville	Jacksonville	Adult
born first-nighter likes to entertain	the very day that I became colored	I am me.

●◆ In a paragraph explain the most important things you learned about Hurston from "How It Feels To Be Colored Me." Speculate on the qualities of character or experiences that might be especially important to her as a writer.

Folklore, Hurston wrote, is the art that people create before they know there is such a thing as art. Folk stories come from people's attempts to understand natural law and the laws of human nature. When given the opportunity to collect **folklore** as part of working on an anthropology degree at Columbia University, Hurston returned to her home in Eatonville where she gathered the folklore of her people. Sitting on porches where people swapped stories, Hurston recorded the talk.

The collection *Mules and Men* has a wide variety of animal tales and **fables**, work songs, fragmentary memories, tales, and folk prescriptions. One type that appears in abundance are stories explaining the origins of natural phenomena or human emotions. As you read one, think about what Hurston learned from these stories that would be useful to her in her own writing.

"How God Made Butterflies" from *Mules and Men* by Zora Neale Hurston

←—Response notes—→

Well, He made butterflies after de world wuz all finished and thru. You know de Lawd seen so much bare ground till He got sick and tired lookin' at it. So God tole 'em to fetch 'im his prunin' shears and trimmed up de trees and made grass and flowers and throwed 'em all over de clearnin's and dey growed dere from memorial days.

Way after while de flowers said, "Wese put heah to keep de world comp'ny but wese lonesome ourselves." So God said, "A world is somethin' ain't never finished. Soon's you make one thing you got to make somethin' else to go wid it. Gimme dem li'l tee-ninchy shears."

So he went 'round clippin' li'l pieces offa everything—de sky, de trees, de flowers, de earth, de varmints and every one of dem li'l clippin's flew off. When folks seen all them li'l scraps fallin' from God's scissors and flutterin' they called 'em flutter-bys. But you know how it is wid de brother in black. He got a big mouf and a stambling tongue. So he got it all mixed up and said, "butter-fly" and folks been calling 'em dat ever since. Dat's how come we got butterflies of every color and kind and dat's why dey hangs 'round de flowers. Dey wu made to keep de flowers company.

207

If you look behind a folk story, it often contains a factual truth (the real event that inspires the story) and an imaginative truth (the meaning created from the real event). In "How God Made Butterflies," the factual truth is that butterflies exist and pollinate flowers. The imaginative truth is the idea that butterflies do this because the flowers are lonely. If you examine how a folk story combines factual and imaginative truth, it is possible to understand how a group of people make sense of themselves and their world.

●◆ Write your own explanation story, such as "Why Trees Have Leaves" or "Why the Sky Is Blue." Use the butterfly story as a model to help you structure a combination of factual and imaginative truth in a way that reflects your cultural heritage.

208

Writers often draw from the storytelling traditions of their own culture for subjects and techniques to use in their own writing.

Creating Characters

Of all Hurston's writing, probably no work is as widely read and studied as her second novel, *Their Eyes Were Watching God*. The novel is an exploration of African American women's developing sense of identity through the main character Janie. She, along with other women characters, is introduced in the opening pages of the novel.

from ***Their Eyes Were Watching God*** by Zora Neale Hurston

←—*Response notes*—→

Ships at a distance have every man's wish on board. For some they come in with the tide. For others they sail forever on the horizon, never out of sight, never landing until the Watcher turns his eyes away in resignation, his dreams mocked to death by Time. That is the life of men.

Now, women forget all those things they don't want to remember, and remember everything they don't want to forget. The dream is the truth. Then they act and do things accordingly.

So the beginning of this was a woman and she had come back from burying the dead. Not the dead of sick and ailing with friends at the pillow and the feet. She had come back from the sodden and the bloated; the sudden dead, their eyes flung wide open in judgment.

The people all saw her come because it was sundown. The sun was gone, but he had left his footprints in the sky. It was the time for sitting on porches beside the road. It was the time to hear things and talk. These sitters had been tongueless, earless, eyeless conveniences all day long. Mules and other brutes had occupied their skins. But now, the sun and the bossman were gone, so the skins felt powerful and human. They became lords of sounds and lesser things. They passed nations through their mouths. They sat in judgment.

Seeing the woman as she was made them remember the envy they had stored up from other times. So they chewed up the back parts of their minds and swallowed with relish. They made burning statements with questions, and killing tools out of laughs. It was mass cruelty. A mood come alive. Words walking without masters; walking altogether like harmony in a song.

"What she doin coming back here in dem overhalls? Can't she find no dress to put on? — Where's dat blue satin dress she left here in? — Where all dat money her husband took and died and left her? — What dat ole forty year ole 'oman doin' wid her hair swingin' down her back lak some young gal? — Where she left dat young lad of a boy she went off here wid? — Thought she was going to marry? — Where he left *her?* — What he done wid all her money? — Betcha he off wid some gal so young she ain't even got no hairs — why she don't stay in her class? —"

from **_Their Eyes Were Watching God_** by Zora Neale Hurston

When she got to where they were she turned her face on the bander log and spoke. They scrambled a noisy "good evenin' " and left their mouths setting open and their ears full of hope. Her speech was pleasant enough, but she kept walking straight on to her gate. The porch couldn't talk for looking.

The men noticed her firm buttocks like she had grape fruits in her hip pockets; the great rope of black hair swinging to her waist and unraveling in the wind like a plume; then her pugnacious breasts trying to bore holes in her shirt. They, the men, were saving with the mind what they lost with the eye. The women took the faded shirt and muddy overalls and laid them away for remembrance. It was a weapon against her strength and if it turned out of no significance, still it was a hope that she might fall to their level some day.

But nobody moved, nobody spoke, nobody even thought to swallow spit until after her gate slammed behind her.

Pearl Stone opened her mouth and laughed real hard because she didn't know what else to do. She fell all over Mrs. Sumpkins while she laughed. Mrs. Sumpkins snorted violently and sucked her teeth.

"Humph! Y'all let her worry yuh. You ain't like me. Ah ain't got her to study 'bout. If she ain't got manners enough to stop and let folks know how she been makin' out, let her g'wan!"

"She ain't even worth talkin' after," Lulu Moss drawled through her nose. "She sits high, but she looks low. Dat's what Ah say 'bout dese ole women runnin' after young boys."

Pheoby Watson hitched her rocking chair forward before she spoke. "Well, nobody don't know if it's anything to tell or not. Me, Ah'm her best friend, and *Ah* don't know."

"Maybe us don't know into things lak you do, but we all know how she went 'way from here and us sho seen her come back. "Tain't no use in your tryin' to cloak no ole woman lak Janie Starks, Pheoby, friend or no friend."

"At dat she ain't so ole as some of y'all dat's talking."

"She's way past forty to my knowledge, Pheoby."

"No more'n forty at de outside."

"She's way too old for a boy like Tea Cake."

"Tea Cake ain't been no boy for some time. He's round thirty his ownself."

"Don't keer what it was, she could stop and say a few words with us. She act like we done something to her," Pearl Stone complained. "She de one been doin' wrong."

"You mean, you mad 'cause she didn't stop and tell us all her business. Anyhow, what you ever know her to do so bad as y'all make out? The worst thing Ah ever knowed her to do was taking a few years offa her age and dat ain't never harmed nobody. Y'all makes me tired. De way you talkin' you'd think de folks in dis town didn't do nothin' in de bed 'cept praise de Lawd. You have to 'scuse me, 'cause Ah'm bound to go take her some supper." Pheoby stood up sharply.

from ***Their Eyes Were Watching God*** by Zora Neale Hurston

←—Response notes—→

"Don't mind us," Lulu smiled, "just go right ahead, us can mind yo' house for you till you git back. Mah supper is done. You bettah go see how she feel. You kin let de rest of us know."

"Lawd," Pearl agreed, "Ah done scorched-up dat lil meat and bread too long to talk about. Ah kin stay 'way from home long as Ah please. Mah husband ain't fussy."

"Oh, er, Pheoby, if youse ready to go, Ah could walk over dere wid you," Mrs. Sumpkins volunteered, "It's sort of duskin' down dark. De booger man might ketch yuh."

"Naw, Ah thank yuh. Nothin' couldn't ketch me dese few steps Ah'm goin'. Anyhow mah husband tell me say no first class booger would have me. If she got anything to tell yuh, you'll hear it."

Pheoby hurried on off with a covered bowl in her hands. She left the porch pelting her back with unasked questions. They hoped the answers were cruel and strange. When she arrived at the place, Pheoby Watson didn't go in by the front gate and down the palm walk to the front door. She walked around the fence corner and went in the intimate gate with her heaping plate of mulatto rice. Janie must be round that side.

She found her sitting on the steps of the back porch with the lamps all filled and the chimneys cleaned.

"Hello, Janie, how you comin'?"

"Aaw, pretty good, Ah'm tryin' to soak some uh de tiredness and de dirt outa mah feet." She laughed a little.

"Ah see you is. Gal, you sho looks *good*. You looks like youse yo' own daughter." They both laughed. "Even wid dem overhalls on, you shows yo' womanhood."

"G'wan! G'wan! You must think Ah brought yuh somethin'. When Ah ain't brought home a thing but mahself."

"Dat's a gracious plenty. Yo' friends wouldn't want nothin' better."

"Ah takes dat flattery offa you, Pheoby, 'cause Ah know it's from de heart." Janie extended her hand "Good Lawd, Pheoby! ain't you never goin' tuh gimme dat lil rations you brought me? Ah ain't had a thing on mah stomach today exceptin' mah hand." They both laughed easily. "Give it here and have a seat."

"Ah knowed you'd be hungry. No time to be huntin' stove wood after dark. Mah mulatto rice ain't so good dis time. Not enough bacon grease, but Ah reckon it'll kill hongry."

211

In the chart, list what you learned about the porch watchers, Pheoby, and Janie through Hurston's **characterizations**. In the middle column, describe how Hurston gives you the information—that is, the techniques she uses to reveal what these women are like. These techniques include: descriptions of appearance, references to their actions, and what they say or what is said about them. In the right column, explain what is revealed about the way they see others and the world.

Characters	What I Know about Them	Techniques of Characterization	What is Revealed
Porch Watchers	critical of Janie	Can't she find no dress to put on?	Jealous of her youthfulness
Pheoby			
Janie			

212

●◆ In a few sentences, summarize what you've learned about:

The porch watchers

Pheoby

Janie

Discuss with others what you learned about these women characters.

●✦ Write a paragraph describing how Hurston characterizes the women, using your chart to support your opinions with specifics. From her characterizations, determine what qualities in women Hurston admires and why.

Writers often express their opinions about the qualities of character they admire through the portrayals they present in fiction.

Hurston made the decision to present multiple **points of view** in *Their Eyes Were Watching God*. At the beginning of the novel, Hurston uses a narrator to give information, but we also hear the voices and thoughts of the characters. In chapter two, however, an **omniscient narrator** tells Janie's story without the interruption of **dialogue** or conversation. As you read the following excerpt, think about the effect of having this omniscient voice tell Janie's story rather than Janie telling it to Pheoby in her own words.

from ***Their Eyes Were Watching God*** by Zora Neale Hurston

← *Response notes* →

Pheoby's hungry listening helped Janie to tell her story. So she went on thinking back to her young years and explaining them to her friend in soft, easy phrases while all around the house, the night time put on flesh and blackness.

She thought awhile and decided that her conscious life had commenced at Nanny's gate. On a late afternoon Nanny had called her to come inside the house because she had spied Janie letting Johnny Taylor kiss her over the gatepost.

It was a spring afternoon in West Florida. Janie had spent most of the day under a blossoming pear tree in the back-yard. She had been spending every minute that she could steal from her chores under that tree for the last three days. That was to say, ever since the first tiny bloom had opened. It had called her to come and gaze on a mystery. From barren brown stems to glistening leaf-buds; from the leaf–buds to snowy virginity of bloom. It stirred her tremendously. How? Why? It was like a flute song forgotten in another existence and remembered again. What? How? Why? This singing she heard that had nothing to do with her ears. The rose of the world was breathing out smell. It followed her through all her waking moments and caressed her in her sleep. It connected itself with other vaguely felt matters that had struck her outside observation and buried themselves in her flesh. Now they emerged and quested about her consciousness.

She was stretched on her back beneath the pear tree soaking in the alto chant of the visiting bees, the gold of the sun and the panting breath of the breeze when the inaudible voice of it all came to her. She saw a dust-bearing bee sink into the sanctum of a bloom; the thousand sister-calyxes arch to meet the love embrace and the ecstatic shiver of the tree from root to tiniest branch creaming in every blossom and frothing with delight. So this was a marriage! She had been summoned to behold a revelation. Then Janie felt a pain remorseless sweet that left her limp and languid.

After a while she got up from where she was and went over the little garden field entire. She was seeking confirmation of the voice and vision, and everywhere she found and acknowledged answers. A personal answer for all other creations except herself. She felt an answer seeking her, but where? When? How? She found herself at the

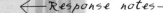

from *Their Eyes Were Watching God* by Zora Neale Hurston

kitchen door and stumbled inside. In the air of the room were flies tumbling and singing, marrying and giving in marriage. When she reached the narrow hallway she was reminded that her grandmother was home with a sick headache. She was lying across the bed asleep so Janie tipped on out of the front door. Oh to be a pear tree—*any* tree in bloom! With kissing bees singing of the beginning of the world! She was sixteen. She had glossy leaves and bursting buds and she wanted to struggle with life but it seemed to elude her. Where were the singing bees for her? Nothing on the place nor in her grandma's house answered her. She searched as much of the world as she could from the top of the front steps and then went on down to the front gate and leaned over to gaze up and down the road. Looking, waiting, breathing short with impatience. Waiting for the world to be made.

Through pollinated air she saw a glorious being coming up the road. In her former blindness she had known him as shiftless Johnny Taylor, tall and lean. That was before the golden dust of pollen had beglamored his rags and her eyes.

In the last stages of Nanny's sleep, she dreamed of voices. Voices far-off but persistent, and gradually coming nearer. Janie's voice. Janie talking in whispery snatches with a male voice she couldn't quite place. That brought her wide awake. She bolted upright and peered out of the window and saw Johnny Taylor lacerating her Janie with a kiss.

215

In this chapter, a **third-person** omniscient (all-knowing) **narrator** tells Janie's story. In the chart below, list the differences in the information that can be learned from a **first-person** and an omniscient narrator. Describe what you think are the differences in purposes and effect of these two points of view.

	purposes	effects
First Person		
Omnisicient		

●◆ In order to examine possible explanations for Hurston's choice of a narrator, select one paragraph from the excerpt from chapter two and rewrite it as if Janie were telling the story directly to Pheoby. Also look back at the excerpt from chapter one (page 209) to understand better how Janie talks. You may choose to have her tell the story with or without the dialect.

Writers use multiple points of view to present a fuller and more complex story.

Hurston grew up surrounded by stories. She wrote that "Men sat around the stores on boxes and benches and passed this world and the next one through their mouths. The right and the wrong, the who, when, and why was passed on, and nobody doubted the conclusions." Hurston began making up stories for herself. "When I began to make up stories I cannot say. Just from one fancy to another, adding more and more detail until they seemed real. People seldom see themselves changing." The stories became Hurston's life work.

➥ Take a look back at the selections you read and determine what ideas and questions are explored in each. Find quotes that best exemplify these themes for you and record them in the chart below.

"How It Feels To Be Colored Me"

ideas:

questions:

"How God Made Butterflies"

ideas:

questions:

Their Eyes Were Watching God

ideas:

questions:

●◆ Examine your chart for similarities and differences in the **central ideas** and questions posed in each selection. Write a short essay describing Hurston's major themes and the meaning that you take away from your reading of Hurston's stories. Include a discussion of what you learned about yourself and others as a result of your reading of her work.

The themes of a writer's work become the basis for readers' explorations of the literary work and their own lives.

Glossary

abstract, existing only as an idea, condition, or feeling that cannot be seen, heard, or touched. Something that is abstract is not CONCRETE.

annotation, a note or comment added to a text to question, explain, or critique the text.

archetype, a SYMBOL, story pattern, THEME, or character type that appear often in literature or art. Archetypes have a universal significance and recognizability. An archetypal character is the damsel in distress.

argument, the ideas or reasoning that hold together a work of literature. *Argument* is generally used in discussion of short poems, particularly the SONNET with its structure.

audience, those people who read or hear what an author has written.

autobiography, an author's account of his or her own life. (See BIOGRAPHY and MEMOIR.)

biography, the story of a person's life written by another person. (See AUTOBIOGRAPHY.)

blank verse, a VERSE FORM consisting of unrhymed IAMBIC PENTAMETER lines. It is the verse form closest to spoken English. Shakespeare's dramas were mostly written in blank verse. (See RHYME.)

central idea, see MAIN IDEA.

characterization, the method an author uses to describe characters and their personalities.

concrete, existing as an actual object that can be seen, heard, or touched. Something that is concrete is not ABSTRACT.

couplet, two LINES of poetry with the same METER. They often RHYME. "I am his Highness' dog at Kew; / Pray tell me, Sir, whose dog are you?" (Alexander Pope)

description, writing that paints a colorful picture of a person, place, thing, or idea using vivid DETAILS.

detail, words from a DESCRIPTION that elaborate on subjects, characters, or action in a work. Details are generally vivid, colorful, and appeal to the senses.

dialogue, the conversation carried on by the characters in a literary work.

diction, an author's choice of words in a literary work.

dimeter, one of the metric lines of poetry. A LINE with two feet is in dimeter. (See METER and FOOT.)

emulation, a copy or IMITATION of a piece of literature, done to practice and study the original.

essay, a type of NONFICTION in which ideas on a single topic are explained, argued, explored, and described. The essay is an immensely varied FORM.

fable, a short, fictional narrative that teaches a lesson. Its characters are generally animals that talk and act like humans.

fact, a thing known to be true or to have actually happened. (See OPINION.)

fiction, PROSE writing that tells an imaginary story. (See NOVEL and SHORT STORY.)

figurative language, language used to create a special effect or feeling. It is characterized by FIGURES OF SPEECH or language that compares, exaggerates, or means something other than what it first appears to mean.

figures of speech, literary devices used to create special effects or feelings. Some common types are METAPHOR, PERSONIFICATION, REPETITION, AND SIMILE.

first-person narrator, See POINT OF VIEW.

folk literature, the various types of ORAL LITERATURE preserved by a culture. Some types of folk literature are FABLES, fairy tales, and myths.

folklore, the traditional beliefs, literature, and customs of a people or culture.

foot, the basic unit of METER. It is a combination of two or three stressed and unstressed syllables. The most common feet are the IAMB and the TROCHEE. (See STRESS.)

219

form, the structure or organization a writer uses for a literary work. There are a large number of possible forms including FABLE, parable, romance, satire, and farce. (See VERSE FORM.)

free verse, poetry that does not have a regular METER or a RHYME scheme.

generalization, an idea or statement that emphasizes the general characteristics rather than the specific DETAILS of a subject.

genre, a category or type of literature based on its style, form, and content. The major genres are drama, fiction, nonfiction, and poetry.

hexameter, one of the metric lines of poetry. A LINE with six feet is in hexameter. (See METER and FOOT.)

iamb, a metrical FOOT in poetry. It consists of an unstressed syllable followed by a stressed one. *New York* and *repeat* are examples of iambs. (See METER and STRESS.)

imagery, the words or phrases a writer uses to represent objects, feelings, actions, or ideas. Imagery is usually based on sensory DETAILS.

imitation, a piece of literature consciously modeled after an earlier piece. Imitations can be copies done for practice or as a serious homage to a writer. (See EMULATION.)

inference, a reasonable conclusion about a character or event in a literary work drawn from the limited facts made available.

inflection, a change in the tone or the pitch of the voice. The inflection of the voice implies the use of a word. The word *well* can be used as an adjective, noun, or exclamation and is inflected differently with each use.

irony, the use of a word or phrase to mean the exact opposite of its literal or normal meaning.

Italian sonnet (also known as the Petrarchan), a 14-LINE poem broken into two parts—an octave (eight lines) and a sestet (six lines)—usually rhyming *abbaabba cdecde*. The general structure of an Italian sonnet is to present a question in the octave that is resolved in the sestet. (See RHYME and SONNET.)

journal, a daily record of thoughts, impressions, and autobiographical information. A journal can be a source for ideas about writing.

light verse, a flexible term describing poetry that was written without serious intent. It is generally humorous and often satirical. Some types of light verse include the LIMERICK, the epigram, and the parody.

limerick, a five-LINE poem usually rhyming *aabba*, with the first, second, and fifth lines written in TRIMETER and the third and fourth in DIMETER. The limerick is generally witty and nonsensical. Limericks are a type of LIGHT VERSE. (See RHYME.)

limited narrator, a THIRD-PERSON NARRATOR who is telling a story from one character's POINT OF VIEW. (See OMNISCIENT NARRATOR.)

line, the metric form of POETRY, which is generally distinguished from PROSE by being broken into lines. Lines are named according to the number of feet they contain and the pattern of these feet. The principal line lengths are MONOMETER, DIMETER, TRIMETER, TETRAMETER, PENTAMETER, and HEXAMETER. (See METER and FOOT.)

literal, the actual or dictionary meaning of a word. It also refers to the usual meaning of phrases, rather than the imaginative or implied meaning an author may add.

main idea, the central point or purpose in a work of literature. It is often stated in a thesis statement or topic sentence. *Main idea* is more commonly employed in discussing NONFICTION than the other GENRES.

memoir, a type of AUTOBIOGRAPHY, that generally focuses on a specific subject or period rather than the complete story of the author's life.

metaphor, a FIGURE OF SPEECH in which one thing is described in terms of another. The comparison is usually indirect, unlike a SIMILE where it is direct. "My thoughts are sheep, which I both guide and serve." (Sir Philip Sidney's, *Arcadia*)

meter, the pattern of stressed and unstressed syllables in a LINE of poetry. The basic unit of meter is the FOOT. (See STRESS.)

monometer, one of the metric lines of poetry. A LINE with one FOOT is in monometer. (See METER.)

mood, the feeling a piece of literature arouses in the reader. It is reflected by the overall atmosphere of the work. (See TONE.)

motif, a repeated idea or THEME in a work of literature. In *The Adventures of Huckleberry Finn*, Huck is constantly in conflict with the "civilized" world. This conflict becomes one of the work's motifs.

narrator, the person telling the story in a work of literature. (See LIMITED NARRATOR, OMNISCIENT NARRATOR, and POINT OF VIEW.)

nonfiction, prose writing that tells a true story or explores an idea. There are many categories of nonfiction, including AUTOBIOGRAPHY, BIOGRAPHY, and ESSAY. (See GENRE.)

novel, a lengthy fictional story with a plot that is revealed by the speech, action, and thoughts of the characters. Novels differ from SHORT STORIES in being developed in much greater depth and detail. (See FICTION and GENRE.)

objective, NONFICTION writing that relates information in an impersonal manner; without feelings or opinions. (See SUBJECTIVE.)

omniscient narrator, a THIRD-PERSON NARRATOR who is able to see into the minds of all the characters in a literary work, narrating the story from multiple POINTS OF VIEW. (See LIMITED NARRATOR.)

opinion, what one thinks or believes. An opinion is generally based on knowledge, but it is not a FACT.

oral literature, stories composed orally or made up as the author goes along. This is the oldest form of literature and is characterized by REPETITION, patterns, and fluidity. Poetic forms such as the ballad and the epic originated as oral literature.

pentameter, one of the metric lines of poetry. A LINE with five feet is in pentameter. (See METER and FOOT.)

persona, the voice or personality an author assumes for a particular purpose. The speaker of a literary work is the author's persona, but may or may not be anything like the author.

220

personification, a FIGURE OF SPEECH in which an author embodies an inanimate object with human characteristics. "The rock stubbornly refused to move" is an example.

perspective, See POINT OF VIEW.

plot, the action or sequence of events in a story. It is usually a series of related incidents that build upon one another as the story develops.

poetry, a GENRE of writing that is an imaginative response to experience reflecting a keen awareness of language. Poetry is generally characterized by LINES, RHYTHM, and, often, RHYME.

point of view, literary term for the perspective from which a story is told. In the first-person point of view, the story is told by one of the characters: "I was tired, so I took the shortcut through the cemetery." In the third-person point of view, the story is told by someone outside the story: "The simple fact is that he lacked confidence. He would rather do something he wasn't that crazy about doing than risk looking foolish." A third-person narrator can be LIMITED or OMNISCIENT. (See NARRATOR.)

prose, writing or speaking in the usual or ordinary form. Prose is any form of writing that is not POETRY.

quatrain, a STANZA of four LINES. The lines can be in any METER or RHYME scheme.

repetition, a FIGURE OF SPEECH in which a word, phrase, or idea is repeated for emphasis and rhythmic effect in a piece of literature. "Bavarian gentians, big and dark, only dark / darkening the day-time, torch-like with the smoking blueness of Pluto's gloom." (D. H. Lawrence, "Bavarian Gentians")

rhyme, the similarity or likeness of sound existing between two words. *Sat* and *cat* are a perfect rhyme because the vowel sounds and final consonant of each word exactly match. Rhyme is a characteristic of POETRY.

rhythm, the ordered occurrence of sound in POETRY. Regular rhythm is called METER. Poetry without regular rhythm is called FREE VERSE.

setting, the time and place in which the action of a literary work occurs.

Shakespearean sonnet (also known as the Elizabethan), a 14-LINE poem consisting of three QUATRAINS and a final COUPLET. The rhyme scheme is *abab cdcd efef gg*. Usually, the quatrains set forth a question or conflict, which is answered or resolved in the couplet. (See RHYME and SONNET.)

short story, a brief fictional story. It usually contains one major theme and one major character. (See FICTION, GENRE, and NOVEL.)

simile, a FIGURE OF SPEECH in which one thing is likened to another. It is a direct comparison employing the words *like* or *as*. Cicero's "A room without books is like a body without a soul" is an example. (See METAPHOR.)

sonnet, a poem consisting of 14 LINES of IAMBIC PENTAMETER. It is one of the most popular VERSE FORMS in English. There are two main types of sonnets, distinguished by their RHYME schemes and structure: the ITALIAN SONNET and the SHAKESPEAREAN SONNET.

stanza, a group of LINES that are set off to form a division in POETRY. A two-line stanza is called a COUPLET. A four-line stanza is a QUATRAIN.

stress, the vocal emphasis given a syllable or word in a metrical pattern. (See METER.)

structure, See FORM.

style, how an author uses words, phrases, and sentences to form ideas. Style is thought of as the qualities and characteristics that distinguish one writer's work from another's.

subjective, NONFICTION writing that includes personal feelings, attitudes, or OPINIONS. (See OBJECTIVE.)

symbol, a person, place, thing, or event used to represent something else. The *dove* is a symbol of peace. Characters in literature are often symbolic of an idea.

syntax, sentence structure; the order and relationship of words in a sentence.

tetrameter, one of the metric lines of poetry. A LINE with four feet is in tetrameter. (See METER and FOOT.)

theme, the statement about life that a writer is trying to get across in a piece of writing. Lengthy pieces may have several themes. In stories written for children, the theme is generally spelled out at the end. In more complex literature, the theme is implied.

thesis, a statement of purpose, intent, or MAIN IDEA in a literary work.

third-person narrator, See POINT OF VIEW.

tone, a writer's attitude toward the subject. A writer's tone can be serious, sarcastic, solemn, OBJECTIVE, and so on.

trimeter, one of the metric lines of poetry. A LINE with three feet is in trimeter. (See METER and FOOT.)

trochee, a metrical FOOT in poetry. It consists of a stressed syllable followed by an unstressed one. *Falling* and *older* are examples of trochees. (See METER and STRESS.)

verse form, the form taken by the lines of a poem. Some of the common verse forms in English are BLANK VERSE, the COUPLET, the LIMERICK, the QUATRAIN, and the SONNET. (See LINE.)

10 "Digging" from *Poems 1965–1975* by Seamus Heaney. Reprinted by permission of Farrar, Straus & Giroux, Inc. Copyright © 1980 by Seamus Heaney.

11 "Blackberry-Picking" from *Poems 1965–1975* by Seamus Heaney. Reprinted by permission of Farrar, Straus & Giroux, Inc. Copyright © 1980 by Seamus Heaney.

13 "Mid-Term Break" from *Poems 1965–1975* by Seamus Heaney. Reprinted by permission of Farrar, Straus & Giroux, Inc. Copyright © 1980 by Seamus Heaney.

16 "Trout" from *Poems 1965–1975* by Seamus Heaney. Reprinted by permission of Farrar, Straus & Giroux, Inc. Copyright © 1980 by Seamus Heaney.

22 "The Story of Midas" from *The Metamorphoses* by Ovid, translated by Rolfe Humphries. Copyright © 1955 by Indiana University Press. Reprinted by permission of Indiana University Press.

25 Excerpt from *The Forgotten Language: An Introduction to the Understanding of Poems, Fairy Tales, and Myths* by Erich Fromm. Copyright © 1951 by Erich Fromm. Reprinted by permission of Henry Holt and Company, Inc.

26 "First Frost" from *Antiworlds and the Fifth Ace* by Andrei Voznesensky. Edited by Patricia Blake and Max Hayward. Copyright © 1966, 1967 by Basic Books, Inc. Copyright © 1963 by Encounter Ltd. Copyright renewed. Reprinted by permission of Basic Books, a subsidiary of Perseus Books Group, LLC.

27 Excerpt from "The Man to Send Rain Clouds" by Leslie Marmon Silko. Copyright © 1981 by Leslie Marmon Silko. First printed in *Storyteller*. Reprinted with the permission of The Wylie Agency, Inc.

30 "December 2001: The Green Morning" by Ray Bradbury. Copyright © 1950, renewed 1977 by Ray Bradbury. Reprinted by permission of Don Congdon Associates, Inc.

39 From *Beowulf*, translated by Burton Raffel. Translation copyright © 1963 by Burton Raffel. Afterword © 1963 by New American Library. Used by permission of Dutton Signet, a division of Penguin Putnam Inc.

43 Excerpt from *The Odyssey* by Homer, translated by Robert Fitzgerald. Copyright © 1961, 1963 by Robert Fitzgerald. Renewed 1989 by Benedict R. C. Fitzgerald. Reprinted by permission of Vintage Books, a division of Random House, Inc.

44 "Lady Madonna" by John Lennon and Paul McCartney. Copyright © 1968 by Sony/ATV Songs LLC.

46 "A Name Is Sometimes An Ancestor Saying Hi, I'm With You" from *Living By the Word: Selected Writings 1973-1987* by Alice Walker. Copyright © 1986 by Alice Walker. Reprinted by permission of Harcourt Brace & Company.

48 "John Wayne" from *Jacklight* by Louise Erdrich. Copyright © 1984 by Louise Erdrich. Reprinted by permission of Henry Holt and Company, Inc.

51 "Frederick Douglass" by Robert Hayden. Copyright © 1966 by Robert Hayden. Reprinted from *Collected Poems* by Robert Hayden. Frederick Glaysher, editor. Reprinted by permission of Liveright Publishing Corporation.

54, 63 Excerpt from *Blue Highways* by William Least Heat Moon. Copyright © 1982 by William Least Heat Moon. By permission of Little, Brown and Company.

55 Excerpt from *The Edge of the Sea* by Rachel Carson. Copyright © 1955 by Rachel Carson. Renewed 1983 by Roger Christie. Reprinted by permission of Houghton Mifflin Company. All rights reserved.

58 Excerpt from "Freedom and Wilderness" from *The Journey Home* by Edward Abbey. Copyright © 1977 by Edward Abbey. Used by permission of Dutton Signet, a division of Penguin Books USA, Inc.

61 "Mushrooms" from *The Colossus and Other Poems* by Sylvia Plath. Copyright © 1960 by Sylvia Plath. Reprinted by permission of Alfred A. Knopf Inc. Taken from *Collected Poems* by Sylvia Plath. Reprinted by permission of Faber and Faber.

66, 68 Excerpts from *Voices from Vietnam* by Barry Denenberg. Copyright © 1995 by Barry Denenberg. Reprinted by permission of Scholastic Inc.

67 Excerpt from *Intervention* by George McT. Kahin. Copyright © 1986 by George McT. Kahin. Reprinted by permission of Alfred A. Knopf Inc.

68 Excerpt from *Everything We Had: An Oral History of the Vietnam War by 33 Americans Who Fought It* by Al Santoli. Copyright © 1981 by Random House. Reprinted by permission of Random House.

70 Excerpt from *When Heaven and Earth Changed Places* by Le Ly Hayslip. Copyright © 1989 by Le Ly Hayslip and Charles Jay Wurts. Used by permission of Doubleday, a division of Bantam Doubleday Dell Publishing Group, Inc.

74 "The Next Step" from *Unaccustomed Mercy*, W. D. Ehrhart, editor. Published by Texas Tech University Press, 1989. Reprinted by permission of the author.

77 Excerpt from *The Ten Thousand Day War: Vietnam 1945-1975* by Michael Maclear. Copyright © 1981 by Michael Maclear. Reprinted by permission of St. Martin's Press, Inc.

80 "Colors" by Shel Silverstein. Copyright © 1974 by Evil Eye Music, Inc. Used by permission of HarperCollins Publishers.

80 "Defining White" from *Words Under the Words: Selected Poems* by Naomi Shihab Nye. Published by Far Corner Books, Portland, Oregon. Copyright © 1995 by Naomi Shihab Nye. Reprinted by permission of the publisher.

85 Excerpt from *A Natural History of the Senses* by Diane Ackerman. Copyright © 1990 by Diane Ackerman. Adapted by permission of Random House, Inc.

87 "Landscape in Scarlet" from *Platero and I* by Juan Ramón Jiménez, translated by Eloise Roach. Copyright © 1957. Renewed 1985. By permission of the University of Texas Press.

89 "Visions" from *She Had Some Horses* by Joy Harjo. Copyright © 1983 by Thunder's Mouth Press. By permission of Thunder's Mouth Press.

92 Excerpt from *Let Us Now Praise Famous Men* by James Agee. Copyright 1939, 1940 by James Agee. Copyright © 1941 by James Agee and Walker Evans. Copyright © renewed 1969 by Mia Fritsch Agee and Walker Evans. Reprinted by permission of Houghton Mifflin Co. All rights reserved.

95 Excerpt from *Serve it Forth* by M. F. K. Fisher. Reprinted with permission of Macmillan USA, a Simon & Schuster Macmillan Company. Copyright © 1937, 1954 by M. F. K. Fisher.

98 "Bread" from *Good Bones and Simple Murders* by Margaret Atwood. Copyright © 1983, 1992, 1994, by O. W. Toad Ltd. A Nan A. Talese Book. Used by permission of Doubleday, a division of Bantam Doubleday Dell Publishing Group, Inc.

104 From *The Pastures of Heaven* by John Steinbeck. Copyright 1932, renewed © 1960 by John Steinbeck. Used by permission of Viking Penguin, a division of Penguin Putnam Inc.

107 From *Cannery Row* by John Steinbeck. Copyright 1945 John Steinbeck 1945. Renewed © 1973 by Elaine Steinbeck, John Steinbeck IV and Thom Steinbeck. Used by permission of Viking Penguin, a division of Penguin Putnam Inc.

110 From *Of Mice and Men* by John Steinbeck. Copyright 1937, renewed © 1965 by John Steinbeck. Used by permission of Viking Penguin, a division of Penguin Putnam Inc.

112 From *The Grapes of Wrath* by John Steinbeck. Copyright © 1939 renewed © 1967 by John Steinbeck. Used by permission of Viking Penguin, a division of Penguin Putnam Inc.

123 Excerpt from *A Thousand Acres* by Jane Smiley. Copyright © 1991 by Jane Smiley Reprinted by permission of Alfred A. Knopf, Inc.

127 "A Flower in the Outfield" by Steve Wulf. Copyright © 1997 Time, Inc. Reprinted by permission.

132 "The Monkey and the Crocodile" from *Jakarta Tales: Animal Stories*. Copyright © 1912. Renewed 1940. Reprinted by permission of Prentice-Hall, Inc., Englewood Cliffs, NJ.

134 "The Hawk and the Buzzard" from *Mules and Men*. Copyright © 1935 by Zora Neale Hurston. Renewed 1963 by John C. Hurston and Joel Hurston. Reprinted by permission of HarperCollins, Inc.

136 "No Tracks Coming Back" from "Negro Folk Tales From the South" in *The Journal of American Folklore*, 1927. Reprinted by permission of the American Folklore Society.

138 "Anansi and His Visitor, Turtle" from *African Village Folk Tales* by Edna Mason Kaula. Copyright © 1968 by Edna Mason Kaula. Used by permission of Philomel Books, a division of The Putnam Putnam Inc.

141 Excerpt from *Refuge: An Unnatural History* by Terry Tempest Williams. Copyright © 1991 by Terry Tempest Williams. Reprinted by permission of Pantheon Books, a division of Random House.

146 "The Handsomest Drowned Man in the World" from *Leaf Storm and Other Stories* by Gabriel García Márquez. Translated by Gregory Rabassa. Copyright © 1971 by Gabriel García Márquez. Reprinted by permission of HarperCollins Publishers, Inc.

152 "Lot's Wife" from *Selected Poems* by Anna Akhmatova. Reprinted by permission of Random House UK Limited.

153 Genesis, 19: 12–26 from *The Good News Bible: Today's English Version,* second edition. Copyright © 1992 American Bible Society. Published by Thomas Nelson, Inc.

156 "Jack" from *The Complete Poems* by Randall Jarrell. Copyright © 1969 by Mrs. Randall Jarrell. Reprinted by permission of Farrar, Straus & Giroux, Inc.

160 "A Blessing" from *The Branch Will Not Break* by James Wright. Copyright © 1963 by James Wright. Used by permission of the University Press of New England.

162 "Unfolding Bud" by Naoshi Koriyama. Copyright © by The Christian Science Monitor. Reprinted by permission.

164 "A Man" by Nina Cassian. Reprinted with permission of Peter Owen Ltd., London.

167 "Every Good Boy Does Fine" by David Wagoner. Copyright © David Wagoner. Reprinted with permission.

172 "Appointment with Love" by S. I. Kishor. Copyright © Sulamith Ish-Kishor. Used with the permission of her estate.

177 "The Chaser" by John Collier. Reprinted with permission of Harold Matson Company, Inc.

181 "One Perfect Rose" copyright 1926, renewed © 1954 by Dorothy Parker, from *The Portable Dorothy Parker* by Dorothy Parker, introduction by Brendan Gill. Used by permission of Viking Penguin, a division of Penguin Putnam Inc.

183 "In a Poem" from *The Poetry of Robert Frost*, edited by Edward Connery Lathem. Copyright © 1942 by Robert Frost. Copyright © 1970 by Lesley Frost Ballantine. Copyright © 1969 by Henry Holt and Company, Inc. Reprinted by permission of Henry Holt and Company, Inc.

184 "The trouble with a kitten" from *Verses from 1920 On* by Ogden Nash. Copyright © 1955 by Ogden Nash. By permission Little, Brown and Company.

186 "The Illiterate" from *Effort at Speech: New and Selected Poems* by William Meredith. Copyright © by William Meredith. Published by TriQuarterly Books/Northwestern University Press in 1997. All rights reserved. Used by permission of Northwestern University Press and the author.

190 "Pity Me Not" from *Collected Poems* by Edna St. Vincent Millay. Copyright © 1923, 1951 by Edna St. Vincent Millay and Norma Millay Ellis. All rights reserved. Reprinted by permission of Elizabeth Barnett, literary executor.

191 "I Really Do Live by the Sea" by Barbara Greenberg. Copyright © Barbara L. Greenberg. Published by the University of Central Florida Press/Orlando.

194 "The Unknown Citizen" from *Collected Poems* by W. H. Auden, edited by Edward Mendelson. Copyright © 1940 and renewed 1968 by W. H. Auden. Reprinted by permission of Random House, Inc.

196 "You Understand the Requirements" by Lyn Lifshin. Copyright © Lyn Lifshin. Reprinted with permission.

199 From *Einstein's Dreams* by Alan Lightman. Copyright © 1992 by Alan Lightman. Reprinted with permission of Pantheon Books, a division of Random House Inc.

207 From *Mules and Men* by Zora Neale Hurston. Copyright 1935 by Zora Neale Hurston. Copyright renewed 1963 by John C. Hurston and Joel Hurston. Reprinted by permission of HarperCollins Publishers, Inc.

209, 214 Excerpts from *Their Eyes Were Watching God* (pages 1–5 and 10–11) by Zora Neale Hurston. Copyright © 1937 by Harper & Row Publishers, Inc. Renewed 1965 by John C. Hurston and Joel Hurston. Reprinted by permission of HarperCollins Publishers, Inc.

Every effort has been made to secure complete rights and permissions for each literary excerpt presented herein. Updated acknowledgments will appear in subsequent printings.

Design: Christine Ronan Design

Photographs: Unless otherwise noted below, all photographs are the copyrighted work of Mel Hill.

Front and Back cover: Copyright © John Hyde/Bruce Coleman Inc.

9 © David Madison/Bruce Coleman Inc.

21 © SuperStock International

37 © Betsie Van Der Meer/Tony Stone Images

53 © SuperStock International

65 © Yann Layma/Tony Stone Images

79 © Nick Vaccaro/Photonica

91 © Japack/Leo de Wys

103 © Larry Towell

117 © Timothy Shonnard/Tony Stone Images

131 © Art Wolfe/Tony Stone Images

145 © Richard H. Johnston/FPG International

159 © Antonia Deutsch/Tony Stone Images

171 © Tim Flach/Tony Stone Images

183 © SuperStock International

193 © Peter Samuels/Tony Stone Images

203 © Thomas Brase/Tony Stone Images

Picture Research: Feldman and Associates